The Global Public
Management Revolution

DONALD F. KETTL

The Global Public
Management Revolution

Second Edition

BROOKINGS INSTITUTION PRESS
Washington, D.C.

ABOUT BROOKINGS

The Brookings Institution is a private nonprofit organization devoted to research, education, and publication on important issues of domestic and foreign policy. Its principal purpose is to bring the highest quality independent research and analysis to bear on current and emerging policy problems. Interpretations or conclusions in Brookings publications should be understood to be solely those of the authors.

Library of Congress Cataloging-in-Publication data
Kettl, Donald F.
The global public management revolution / Donald F. Kettl.— 2nd ed.
p. cm.
Summary: "Explores the current models of government reform across the world, examining the basic tool kit of reformers and probing the underlying issues of government management and the puzzles of governance in the twenty-first century, with special focus on New Zealand and the United States"—Provided by publisher.
Includes bibliographical references and index.
ISBN-13: 978-0-8157-4919-6 (pbk. : alk. paper)
ISBN-10: 0-8157-4919-8 (pbk. : alk. paper)
1. Public administration. 2. Comparative government. 3. New Zealand—Politics and government—21st century. 4. United States—Politics and government—2001– I. Title.
JF1351.K475 2005   2005015705
352.3'67—dc22

9 8 7 6 5 4 3 2 1

Typeset in Sabon

Composition by R. Lynn Rivenbark
Macon, Georgia

Printed by R. R. Donnelley
Harrisonburg, Virginia

Contents

Preface

If there is any constant in a globalizing world, it is the rapid pace of government change. Virtually every nation in the world is struggling to make its government stronger by increasing the efficiency of its administrative processes and improving its performance. As the second edition of this book shows, a surprising revolution in public management has been sweeping the globe for the last generation, and it shows no sign of flagging.

The defining element of this revolution is the search for stronger results: a government that, in the words of the Clinton administration's "reinventing government" movement, "works better and costs less." A wide array of strategies have been launched to pursue that goal, including New Zealand's "new public management," various American reforms during both Republican and Democratic administrations, and other concerted efforts in developing nations around the world.

Reformers have deployed three broad strategies: modest changes, in nations like France and Germany; incremental reform, in the United States; and "big bang" reform in nations ranging from New Zealand to the Slovak Republic. Crises often have sparked the changes, and sustaining them often has become an enduring problem. Moreover, as a parade of reforms has come and gone in many nations, reform fatigue often has set in.

Nevertheless, despite the wide range of efforts to reform public management, they converge remarkably on a single driving theme: measuring performance, especially program outcomes. Better assess what government does and how well it does it, the underlying philosophy suggests, and it will be easier to hold public administrators accountable for their performance and elected officials accountable for their leadership. The search for better performance and accountability is the core of the instinct for reform. The more complex governmental problems have become—and therefore the more intricate governments' administrative strategies—the more governments' instincts for reform have grown.

However, despite the fundamental focus on management, management reform is not fundamentally about management. Reformers reform because it helps them serve a broader political purpose. Sometimes that broader purpose takes a narrow form, like finding a signature issue on which public officials can campaign for reelection. Sometimes it is an effort to connect with citizens who, throughout the world, often harbor deep distrust about the political process and fight higher taxes. Sometimes it is an effort to improve the accountability of administrators and enhance their control of the programs that they manage. The range of political motivations is wide, but the fundamental fact is that all management reforms have deep political roots and profound political implications. Uncovering those political purposes and discovering how management reforms sometimes support them—and sometimes do not—is the goal of this book.

The first edition of this book grew from discussions at the Global Forum on Reinventing Government in Washington, January 14–15, 1999. That forum brought together public officials from around the world, from Mongolia to the Middle East and from New Zealand to Europe, to explore the fundamental issues and driving trends of the reform movement. Since then, I have had the privilege of continuing those conversations with officials at the World Bank and the Organization for Economic Cooperation and Development, as well as with government officials in many nations around the world. With remarkable energy and enthusiasm, they continue to seek governments that work better, cost less, and connect better with the citizens that they are trying to serve. What appears in the pages of this second edition is an effort to capture the living nature of government reform.

DONALD F. KETTL

June 2005
Philadelphia, Pennsylvania

CHAPTER ONE

Foundations of Reform

Since the 1980s, a remarkable movement to reform public management has swept the globe. In fact, the movement is global in two senses. First, it has spread around the world, from Mongolia, China, and India to Sweden, New Zealand, and the United States. Second, it has been sweeping in scope. Governments have pursued management reform to deliver better value for tax money and, more fundamentally, to reshape the relationship of the state with its citizens. Some nations, such as the United States, have been inveterate reformers, but virtually no part of the planet has escaped the impulse to reform.

The movement has been striking not only in its breadth but also in its common characteristics. In general, it has built on six core components:[1]

—*Productivity.* How can governments produce more services with less tax money? Citizens everywhere have demanded a rollback in taxes, but their taste for government services has scarcely diminished. Governments have had to find ways to squeeze more services from the same—or smaller—revenues.

—*Marketization.* How can government use market-style incentives to root out the pathologies of its bureaucracy? Some governments have privatized extensively by selling public enterprises, whereas others have relied heavily on contracting out to nongovernmental partners for service delivery. In both cases, they have struggled to change the fundamental incentives of government bureaucracy. Underlying those tactics is a basic strategy: replace the traditional command-and-control mechanism with a market mechanism and then rely on the market mechanism to change the behavior of government managers.

—*Service orientation.* How can government better connect with citizens? Public opinion polls show that public trust in government institutions has declined and that many citizens believe that government programs are unresponsive. To make programs more responsive, governments have tried to turn their service delivery systems upside down. Instead of designing programs from the point of view of service providers (especially government officials) and managing them through existing bureaucratic structures, reformers have tried to put citizens (as service recipients) first. In some cases, this strategy has meant giving citizens a choice among alternative service systems. In others, it has meant training program managers to focus on improving service. Markets naturally provide consumers with choice. Government reformers have used market mechanisms to give citizens the same choice—or at least to encourage a customer-oriented approach to providing service.

—*Decentralization.* How can government make programs more responsive and effective? Many nations have devolved responsibility for various programs to lower levels of government. In some federal systems (for example, those of Australia, Canada, Switzerland, and the United States), this strategy has meant shifting power within the system. In other nations, it has meant transferring more responsibility for service delivery to local governments. Some governments also have devolved responsibility within public agencies to increase frontline managers' incentives and ability to respond to citizens' needs.

—*Policy.* How can government improve its capacity to devise and track policy? Many governments, following the lead of New Zealand, have explicitly separated government's role in purchasing services (its policy-making function) from its role in providing them (its service delivery function). Those governments have sought to improve the efficiency of service delivery, which might or might not remain in the hands of government, while improving their oversight capacity.

—*Accountability.* How can governments improve their ability to deliver what they promise? Governments have tried to replace top-down, rule-based accountability systems with bottom-up, results-driven systems. They have sought to focus on outputs and outcomes instead of processes and structures.

Painted with the broadest brush, these reforms have sought to replace traditional rule-based, authority-driven processes with market-based, competition-driven tactics. Indeed, many nations with substantial state-owned enterprises (such as telephone, airline, and power generation companies) have sold them to move them into the private market. But the global reform process is much more than a simple effort to replace bureaucratic processes with markets. It has been shaped by a fundamental effort to transform government itself.

The Transformation of Public Management

What explains the fact that so many governments pursued such similar strategies so aggressively at much the same time? Four forces have played a part:

—*Political.* Following the end of the cold war, many nations found themselves wrestling with a fundamental debate about the role of government. In nations that once lay behind the Iron Curtain, governments had the daunting task of transforming their basic systems of governance, devising institutions that were more democratic, building civil society, and reshaping their relationships with citizens. Indeed, some of those nations, like the Slovak Republic, quickly became some of the world's most aggressive and imaginative reformers. One Slovak official, in fact, referred to his nation's efforts as "modernization on steroids."[2] Developing nations, facing strong calls to modernize their economies quickly, found themselves under quite similar pressures. Their citizens, looking at the pace of economic growth elsewhere, have put tremendous pressure on elected officials to catch up. Meanwhile, industrialized nations have had to cope with an increasingly global economy. And nations everywhere have had to confront a darker aspect of globalization. Participation in the global economy brings with it the inescapable risk of terrorist threats, a risk that requires nations to fashion effective systems of homeland security.

Political candidates the world over have waged successful campaigns on the theme of how to shrink government and improve public services. Even in large welfare states like Denmark and Sweden, the currents of reform have been strong. Public officials have seen real value in promising to put a lid on government spending, but they have struggled to cope with citizens' demands for public services. Those demands have hardly shrunk, so elected officials have relied on management reform to try to solve the conundrum.

—*Social*. Some nations have undergone profound societal transformation. In South Africa, for example, the end of apartheid required the government to find ways to bring disenfranchised blacks into political life. Many eastern European nations have been working to reconstruct their social, legal, economic, and political systems. In many industrialized nations, standards of living have stagnated, and families have increasingly required two wage earners to attain the standard of living to which they aspire. Finally, societies everywhere have struggled to cope with the radical shift from the Industrial Age to the Information Age. Ideas have spread with stunning speed. Companies—and nations—that have failed to keep up have been punished quickly and harshly. These transformations have created a strong impetus for reform.

—*Economic*. In the late 1990s, the Asian financial crisis, among others, profoundly challenged the financial structure of East Asian nations. After years of "Asian miracles," economic calamities gave rise to great urgency for reform. Other nations, such as New Zealand and the United Kingdom, launched their reforms to escape economic stagnation and spark economic growth. Corporate leaders in many nations have complained that government, especially through its tax and regulatory policies, has reduced economic growth and limited the global competitiveness of their businesses. Deregulation, privatization, and other tactics to promote job creation and economic growth became central to the debate.

—*Institutional*. All governments have found themselves part of an increasingly global economy and political environment. Major initiatives— military, economic, and political—require careful negotiations and reliable partnerships. Within the European Union, nations are racing to create supranational structures to harmonize their government policies and improve their economic performance. Meanwhile, international organizations, including the United Nations, the World Bank, the International Monetary Fund, the Inter-American Development Bank, and the World Trade Organization, are playing a big role in shaping the world community. Nongovernmental organizations have become vastly more numerous and increasingly important in shaping both political debate and service delivery. Many national governments have devolved more decisionmaking to the local level. Political power and program administration have simultaneously become more concentrated at the supranational level and less concentrated in subnational governments and civil society. The result is a new constellation of relationships that are increasingly important but not well understood.

Reform and Governance

As nations have struggled to deal with these problems, the reform movement has spread like wildfire. Indeed, the movement has become so widespread—and chic—that no self-respecting central government can be seen as *not* having some sort of reform underway, no matter how modest. Ideas have driven action, but public officials have rarely stopped to assess how well reforms have worked elsewhere or to determine the preconditions required to achieve the results that they have observed. In fact, the results often have been very modest.[3] This observation frames a profound paradox: government management is both more and less important than the reform movement suggests.

On one hand, macrogovernance and macroeconomic issues often swamp management reform. What usually matters most, to elected officials and citizens alike, is whether the economy is growing, producing new jobs and a higher quality of life. New Zealanders tend to gauge the success of their nation's reforms by how long they have to wait for medical procedures. Swedes assess their reforms by the level of economic growth, continued provision of treasured social welfare programs, and maintenance of social cohesion. Al Gore spent eight years championing the Clinton administration's efforts to reinvent the U.S. federal government. He got no political payoff for the effort that he put into the campaign (or for the sustained economic success of the Clinton years). Gore lost the election because George W. Bush succeeded in framing larger anti-Clinton political issues, from a promise to restore integrity to a pledge for greater collaboration between the parties, and took the reform issue away from him.

On the other hand, the performance of government bureaucracies increasingly plays a central role in the macro-level political and economic issues that elected officials—and voters—do care about. To keep services high and taxes low, governments must manage their debt and public programs effectively. Government managers and elected officials alike have frequently complained that standard bureaucratic procedures often handicap their government's ability to respond effectively to global challenges.

Hence government reform is often much more important than it appears on the surface. Without strong public management well-equipped to tackle the problems that government faces, governments in many nations have been unable to play their required roles.

Moreover, in countries around the world, government action depends increasingly on nongovernmental partners, from nongovernmental organizations that deliver public services to private contractors who supply important goods. In order to embrace the large and complex networks responsible for service delivery, many reformers now speak of *governance* instead of government. As these networks have become more important, government officials have increasingly reached out to sweep them into the reform movement as well. Improving government services requires more than managing government agencies.

In short, as I suggest in this volume, the most important aspect of the global reform movement in public management is the fact that public management is only part of the picture. The movement's central problems revolve around government's relationship with civil society. The strategies and tactics of government reform seek to strengthen government's capacity to meet citizens' hopes. The success or failure of the movement depends on how deeply its reforms become wired into a nation's systems of governance—in its political institutions, for-profit and not-for-profit partnerships, public expectations, and civil society.

In fact, the global public management movement is part of a fundamental debate about governance. The implicit assumption is that the government of the past century will not suffice to tackle the problems of the next—that government needs to be reinvented and transformed to deal effectively with the problems of the twenty-first century. What should government do? How can it best accomplish its goals? What capacity does it need to do its job well? What should be the relationship between the nation-state and multinational organizations? What should be the relationship between nation-states and subnational governments, the private sector, and nongovernmental organizations? How can government best promote democratic accountability? How can the emerging structures and relationships promote the interests of citizens as a whole and escape capture by narrow interests? How can citizen distrust and alienation be minimized? The management reform movement builds on the notion that good governance—a sorting out of mission, role, capacity, and relationships—is a necessary (if insufficient) condition for economic prosperity and social stability.

The pages that follow explore the basic models of reform, especially in New Zealand and the United States. They examine the basic tool kit of reformers, in these nations and around the world, and probe the underlying issues of government management and the large puzzles of governance in the twenty-first century.

CHAPTER TWO

Reform, Westminster Style

The transformation of governance has produced a reform movement as varied as the nations of the world. South Koreans have debated whether there is a distinct Asian cultural and political identity and whether such an identity would require reforms to be carefully tailored to the region. The Mexican government has launched a twin-edged movement to improve efficiency and reduce corruption. Finland has strengthened its management-by-results system. The Danes have launched a major initiative to rethink the capacity of their top-level government managers to deliver results. The Americans have "reinvented" their government, and the United Kingdom has launched multiple stages of government reform. Less developed countries frequently have found themselves whipsawed between pressure to copy the well-known reforms of some developed countries and the need to build basic management capacity beforehand. Even though multinational organizations have struggled to define which strategies are most likely to be effective, they often have made management reform a precondition for aid. Everyone is doing it, but there is no consensus on what ought to be done—on what reforms work best, what problems can be solved through reform, and what the inherent limits of reform are.

Portions of chapters 2 and 3 have been adapted from my chapter in *Institutions of American Democracy: The Executive Branch*, edited by Joel Auerbach and Mark Peterson (Oxford University Press, 2005), by permission of Oxford University Press and the Annenberg Foundation Trust at Sunnylands.

Reform efforts around the world have fallen roughly into two broad models: Westminster reforms, the pathbreaking efforts of governments in New Zealand and the United Kingdom (named for the palace that houses the British government); and American-style reform, which has been more incremental yet, paradoxically, more sweeping than Westminster-style reform. This chapter examines the Westminster reforms. The next chapter assesses the American reforms.

New Zealand first demonstrated the cutting-edge Westminster approach, which has since spread to other Westminster-style governments, including those of Australia and Canada. It defined a "new public management" aimed at shrinking the size of—and imposing market-style discipline on—government. The United States, by contrast, came relatively late to the global movement. Its "reinventing government" strategy, along with that strategy's successors, has produced less fundamental restructuring but more sweeping administrative changes. These two strategies define the basic models, which have powerfully shaped debate around the world.

Managerialism: Westminster-style Reforms

Modern public management reform had its true start in New Zealand in the late 1970s and early 1980s. Indeed, no government has traveled farther or faster in reshaping its public programs or management systems. The changes were remarkable not only for their scale but also for their strategic focus. The reformers relied on the Chicago School of neoclassical economics to devise a plan for reforming the New Zealand public sector. Chicago School economists were highly suspicious of government's ability to shape the economy; instead, they called for reliance on the free market. Market incentives, they believed, produced far more efficient decisions (and therefore better results) than government control ever could. When government needed to be involved, the Chicago School believed that market-like incentives ought to shape the behavior of government bureaucrats.[1]

The New Zealand government traditionally had been one of the most proactive in the world in terms of expanding basic rights and government programs; for example, it was the first country to grant women the right to vote (in 1893).[2] It later created the world's first "cradle-to-grave" welfare system (in 1935) and evolved into one of the most aggressive welfare states in the world, with a large public sector that provided a wide range of services to citizens. Its "cocoon economy," as analyst Allen Schick christened it, helped sustain the system.[3] There was little unemployment or inflation, and the standard of living ranked among the world's highest. The economy was highly regulated and subsidized. State-owned enterprises, from transportation and energy to communications companies, dominated public spending.

However, by the early 1980s the New Zealand economy could no longer support the nation's ambitious public programs. Faced with tough competition from the emerging Pacific Rim economies and declining agricultural trade with the United Kingdom, the country found itself in economic chaos. The economy stagnated and inflation soared. Traditional pump-priming strategies failed to stimulate the economy and instead fueled inflation, which led to a run on the New Zealand dollar. The size of the problem, coupled with declining confidence in Keynesian economics and other forms of government intervention in the economy, set the stage for a radical transformation of the nation's public sector.

The economic crisis cost the National Party its parliamentary majority and brought the Labour Party to power in July 1984, for the first time in nine years. Heading the Finance Ministry in the new government was Roger Douglas, a devotee of the Chicago School of economics who pressed for massive changes in government policy and management. The market-based approach drove his strategy, which was characterized by a commitment to competition, a belief in using market processes to shape the incentives of government employees, and a view of reform that was heavily influenced by new institutional economic theories. His approach, quickly christened "Rogernomics," drew first on ideas about transaction costs: the high cost of gathering information about policies strengthens the power of special interests and increases the chance that those interests will capture the attention of decisionmakers.[4] Effective reform requires finding a way for government policymakers to break that connection. It also drew on the theory of the agency problem: policy management requires policymakers to delegate responsibility to low-level officials through a kind of contract: work is delivered in exchange for salary payments. However, effectively supervising those employees is very costly, because it is difficult to define tasks clearly, monitor results, and enforce the contracts. As several former New Zealand government officials explained, "The goal for designers of public sector institutions and processes is to avoid public choice problems and minimize agency costs."[5]

The New Zealand reformers drew on a multipart, top-down strategy that sought to privatize public programs wherever possible. For example, they moved to sell the state-owned airline and other public services to private sector owners, and they sought to substitute market incentives for command-and-control bureaucratic practices. Top agency managers, for example, were hired under contracts; they could receive substantial rewards for good performance—or they could be fired if they did not perform. The reformers also sought to focus single-mindedly on outputs instead of inputs, especially budgets. They wanted to move government to focus more on results. They sought nothing less than a complete revolution in what the government did and how it did it—and in the process they fundamentally rewove the very fabric of the New Zealand government. Schick, in the most comprehensive and incisive analysis of the reforms in New Zealand, called it "a singular accomplishment in the development of modern public administration."[6]

The reformers coupled their economic theories with management reform ideas borrowed from the private sector, where corporate managers were preaching that employees could not manage effectively unless they had the flexibility to determine the best way to meet policy goals. Douglas and colleagues agreed that managers ought to be held responsible for results. Managers therefore needed the freedom to spend within their budgets, to hire the best employees to do the job, and to buy the supplies and equipment they needed for the tasks at hand. Traditional New Zealand administration had imposed heavy controls on public managers, giving them little freedom. The reformers have sought, in short, to balance two competing approaches: giving managers more flexibility ("letting the managers manage," as they say in New Zealand) while holding them strictly accountable for results ("making the managers manage").

Two remarkable features characterized this effort. First, powerful theories guided the reform strategy; second, those theories shaped the thinking of officials throughout the government. The formal language of transaction cost economics spread out from the Treasury to government offices throughout Wellington, and soon high-level discussions about this abstract theory became as common as those about the substance of government programs. The Labour Party government made the reform the centerpiece of its ambitious and aggressive campaign to reshape public management, and even Chicago School economists were surprised at how their ideas had penetrated the nation's government.

The New Zealand Strategy

The New Zealand reforms were not so much a single effort as a composite undertaking that evolved over more than fifteen years. Indeed, June Pallot identified four different stages of reform. The managerialist phase (1978–85) introduced private sector–style management (including accrual accounting) into government operations. The marketization phase (1986–91) brought economic approaches to government management, including contracts, market competition, and incentives based on individual self-interest. During the strategic phase (1992–96), the government sought to provide a comprehensive overview of government programs to reduce the fragmentation encouraged by marketization. In the adaptive capacity phase (1997 onward), the government concentrated on developing the capability to manage the new strategies, especially in human resources.[7]

These reforms have been the world's most aggressive and ambitious. Together, they present a comprehensive and theory-driven package of ideas. The reformers sought first to increase the transparency of government by clearly specifying the goals of government programs and reporting on their results. They separated the purchase and production functions. The government would decide what should be done and then rely on whoever could do the job most effectively and cheaply. After elected officials made basic policy decisions, government managers had great discretion over how best to do the job. Cabinet officials hired chief executives under fixed-term contracts and performance-based incentives to implement programs. The contracts specified outputs (for example, miles of roadway to be built or number of children to be vaccinated), held the chief executives responsible for delivering those outputs, and rewarded them according to how well they accomplished the task.

In general, the reformers tried to separate policymaking from policy administration, replace traditional government bureaucracy and authority with market-driven competition and incentives, make goals and outputs transparent, and give government managers flexibility in determining how to reach those goals. The reforms were not explicitly antigovernmental and did not set out to reshape government operations. Rather, the reformers sought to reduce the scope of government functions, to determine how best to perform them—within government or outside it—and to use results as the ultimate measure of performance. The New Zealand initiative comprised several common threads:

—*Privatization and corporatization.* The New Zealand government privatized many state-owned, state-run services (including telephone, post office, airline, and oil companies). In all, the government sold more than twenty state-owned companies.[8] However, privatization itself was not nearly as important as a broader effort to increase the productivity of state-owned enterprises. The government viewed those enterprises as entities in which it held an ownership interest, and its role was to ensure the maximum return for taxpayers. The 1986 State-Owned Enterprises Act, which wrote those principles into law, was one of the first and most important pieces of New Zealand reform legislation.

—*Performance contracting.* The 1988 State Sector Act and the 1989 Public Finance Act cemented the reforms in government's core departments. The acts gave chief executives great flexibility in hiring, firing, and paying their employees. The New Zealand government made output-based contracts between government officials and government managers the keystone of its reforms, and the chief executives themselves moved from lifetime tenure to five-year contracts.

—*Output budgeting.* The 1988 State Sector Act made government managers responsible for performance. In particular, the act sought to move accountability from inputs (resources used, especially tax dollars) to outputs (the activity—and the quality of the activity—produced). Many government programs work through administrative intermediaries or depend on social factors for their success. The success of social welfare programs, for example, can depend as much on the performance of the economy (how easy it is to move people from public assistance to private employment) as on how well the programs work. The New Zealand reformers have insisted, however, that government managers be held accountable for the results that they can control.

—*Strategic planning.* Since 1992 the New Zealand government has been producing comprehensive accrual budgets. Most governments keep their books on a cash basis—that is, tallying tax dollars collected each year minus government expenditures in the same year. New Zealand became the world's first government to use the accrual method to assess the full cost of its programs, including the long-term cost of commitments already made. Government officials had carefully read the economic theories regarding government decisionmaking, and they concluded that cash accounting created strong incentives for making decisions today whose full cost would not be borne until much later. Accrual accounting forced them to deal with the full cost of decisions as they made them. Moreover,

the Fiscal Responsibility Act of 1994 mandated that the government identify its fiscal objectives and report on how well it achieved them.

The government then mandated the creation of strategic result areas
(SRAs) and key result areas (KRAs). Government officials were required
to move from establishing broad policy goals to specifying the strategies
that agencies would pursue to attain them, and those strategies would
determine the SRAs on which the agencies would focus over the coming
three to five years. The cabinet defined the SRAs, which became binding
on the cabinet departments. The SRAs then shaped budget decisions and
the specific outputs required of chief executives—the KRAs—in their contracts. The SRAs and KRAs not only shape the budget and accounting
systems but also define basic accountability in New Zealand government—who does what—and how the different pieces fit together to form
government policy.

As the government has begun to discuss cross-cutting strategies explicitly, government officials have been forced to step back and ponder two
related issues. First, market-driven processes risk atomizing government
programs. Officials are principally responsible for producing the outputs
defined in their contracts, not necessarily for how well their programs
connect with others. New Zealanders have begun exploring the broader
implications of government policy—how outputs cumulate into outcomes. Second, government officials in particular worry about their
capacity for taking on the vastly new challenges of managing the reforms.
Indeed, Schick pointed out in his seminal study of the New Zealand
reforms that these issues represent puzzles to which the government must
turn next as the spirit of reform continues.[9]

Evolution of the New Zealand Reforms

It is hardly surprising that the New Zealand reforms have continued to
evolve. The basic New Zealand strategy envisioned a highly fragmented
government sector in order to allow careful assignment of accountability,
create effective incentives for high performance, and permit systematic
measurement of outputs. However, that approach came under heavy fire
following a tragic accident that occurred in April 1995, when seventeen
students crowded onto a viewing platform above Cave Creek, a scenic
area on the country's west coast. Several students began shaking the platform—"just fooling around," as one of them later recalled. "It was shaking a lot. We were giving it a good nudge. But we felt safe doing it." With-

out warning, however, "There was a sudden movement forward and the platform just dropped. It tilted in a violent movement, and we all fell forward against the handrail." The platform collapsed and fell almost 100 feet into a gully. Fourteen people died.[10]

For New Zealanders, the accident had wrenching consequences. A subsequent investigation revealed that the platform had been poorly designed and that the staff building the platform did not have adequate qualifications. But in the end, no individual officials were held accountable. That led to searching questions. The New Zealand reforms had been designed to produce efficient, effective services and to hold officials accountable for high performance. But the system had allowed a substandard platform to be built without anyone being ultimately held responsible. Many New Zealanders concluded that the reforms needed fundamental reform: that the system was too fragmented and too often coordination suffered as a result; that there was not sufficient focus on responsiveness to citizens; that the focus on outputs (the activities of public managers) neglected the assessment of outcomes (the impact of those activities); and that the government was dedicating insufficient attention to developing a cadre of skilled managers. As Michael Wintringham, New Zealand's State Services Commissioner, explained in 2001,

> I find it extraordinary that we have, for so long, clung to a belief that a decentralised system, with wide autonomy, different standards and approaches applying across 38 departments, with minimum rewards and sanctions, with a focus on annual delivery at the expense of long-run investment generally, will deliver people with strong, shared values, with a keen sense of belonging to the Public Service and with the skills and attributes needed to lead the Public Service for another decade. I don't think it makes sense.[11]

Soon after a center-left coalition government won election in 1999, the New Zealand reforms underwent a significant reassessment. The government launched a new initiative called Strengthening the Centre that focused on "doing the right things and doing them right."[12] The effort asserted, in brief, that "New Zealand's system of public management should provide an holistic, transparent and appropriate mandate for the exercise of leadership on whole-of-government matters across the various parts of the broader State sector."[13] It sought to move New Zealand's government system from fragmentation to integration, from outputs to outcomes, from private sector–style incentives to a focus on public interest and civic capacity. Efforts to distinguish between the core public sector and the broader effort to harness private sector–style enterprises to do government's work became known to many citizens as the "Wellington waffle."[14] The government remained committed to reform, but it focused on reforms designed to integrate government services more effectively— to deliver value for taxpayers' dollars while enhancing government's capacity to assess the results that citizens care about most.

Reform the Westminster Way

The New Zealand reforms represent only one of many ambitious movements in countries with British-style parliamentary systems. Australia mounted a similarly strong reform effort. Unlike the New Zealand reforms, which drew heavily on economic theories to transform incentives ("making the managers manage"), the Australian reforms focused on removing barriers to effective administration ("letting the managers manage").[15] The Australians focused earlier than the New Zealanders did on paying more attention to outcomes. Canada also undertook extensive reforms to shrink the size of government and to improve the coordination of public services.[16]

In the Westminster world the New Zealand reforms remain the most comprehensive and aggressive effort, even though the British reforms are perhaps better known. Whereas the New Zealand reforms were launched from the left, the British reforms grew from the right, with Prime Minister Margaret Thatcher's Financial Management Initiative, a neoconservative venture to shrink the size of the state. Launched in 1982, the initiative centered on separating the government's functions into clear responsibility centers, identifying the costs (on an accrual basis) associated with producing outputs in each center, and holding managers strictly accountable for results. This initiative drew heavily on private sector approaches to production, and later strategies incorporated a heavy customer service component into the production function. British "citizens' charters," for example, set service standards for government programs. As part of the Next Steps initiative, many government bureaucracies were spun off into separate agencies that operated under contract to the parent department for the production of specified outputs in exchange for greater flexibility in using resources. Officials used "market testing"—privatizing public services where possible and subjecting remaining public services to market competition—to improve the incentives for efficiency.[17]

In many of the Westminster nations, officials worked to enhance service coordination. The Blair government in the United Kingdom, for example, promoted a strategy of "joined-up government," whereby the government would no longer expect citizens to find their way to the right office. Instead, the government committed itself to presenting citizens with "no wrong door": the government would be organized to ensure that its agents could manage citizens' needs, regardless of how and where citizens encountered the government. Information technology, for example, would be used to create a more seamless link between government agencies and the people that they served. The British government also moved more toward assessment of outcomes. The Westminster nations had hardly lost their taste for reform, but their commitment to the Chicago School diminished considerably. Private markets continued to play an important role in service delivery, but governments worked hard to enhance their control of the service delivery system.

The New Public Management

Together, the British Commonwealth experiments amounted to a "new public management," said analysts.[18] The movement produced a commitment to "managerialism," which Christopher Pollitt called the "seldom-tested assumption that better management will prove an effective solvent for a wide range of economic and social ills."[19] The new public management stemmed from the basic economic argument that government suffered from the defects of monopoly, high transaction costs, and information problems that bred great inefficiencies. By substituting market competition—and market-like incentives—the reformers believed that they could shrink government's size, reduce its costs, and improve its performance. Perhaps surprisingly, the movement did not have clear ideological roots. Sometimes the argument came from the left, as in New Zealand; sometimes it came from the right, as in the United Kingdom. However, at its core the movement sought to transform how government performed its most basic functions.

Many analysts have questioned whether the new public management is real, whether its underlying market philosophy is valid, and whether it has truly accomplished what it has claimed. Indeed, Laurence E. Lynn Jr. has asked whether the new public management has truly transformed

government's core functions. He contends that "there is no new paradigm" shaping theory and practice.[20]

Even if the jury is still out on the long-range impact of the managerial
movement, its first two decades established clear changes in the Westminster governments. Sandford Borins has identified the following characteristic components:[21]

—*Customer service.* Broad initiatives have been implemented to improve the responsiveness of public programs.

—*Operating autonomy.* Government functions have been separated
into quasi-autonomous agencies to give managers more flexibility in pursuing their goals (especially in budget and human resource policies).

—*Output measurement.* A results-based measurement system has been
created in which both agencies and senior managers work under performance contracts. (However, performance-based pay seems not to have
worked.)

—*Human resources.* Downsizing and pay freezes have hurt employee
morale; however, governments are seeking to improve recruitment and
training packages to bolster the workforce.

—*Information technology.* Extensive use of information technology to
improve service delivery has created a new generation of policy issues,
from access to privacy concerns, that governments must resolve.

—*Privatization.* Operations have been spun off to the private sector
where possible, and new service delivery partnerships have been developed with private and nonprofit organizations.

Scholars may continue to question whether these features represent a
new paradigm, but there is little doubt that the Westminster reforms have
become the touchstone in the global debate about what government
does—and how it can do it better.

CHAPTER THREE

Reform,
American Style

American government came to the management reform movement much later than the Westminster governments. As government spending rose after World War II, government officials and their critics struggled with new puzzles. How could the nation ensure that government programs worked? How could programs be made both effective and accountable? In tackling those problems, two commissions headed by former president Herbert Hoover had an enormous impact on thinking about how government could best do its work. They also marked an important transition in that thinking. The first Hoover Commission concentrated on the structure of government, and the second Hoover Commission shifted its focus to government processes. That transition guided most of the government reform movement for the rest of the twentieth century.

In the academic world, the questions about government performance proved so tough that they gave rise to a new subfield of political science called "implementation." This area of research was rooted in public policy and dedicated to understanding why so many programs seemed to work so poorly—or, as the discursive subtitle of a book by Jeffrey L. Pressman and Aaron Wildavsky soberly put it, to understanding "How Great Expectations in Washington Are Dashed in Oakland; Or, Why It's Amazing That Federal Programs Work at All, This Being a Saga of the Economic Development Administration as Told by Two Sympathetic Observers Who Seek to Build Morals on a Foundation of Ruined Hopes."[1] Reformers worried that federal grant programs administered through state and local governments had produced inflexible approaches that poorly matched local problems and gave too little power to those in the areas most affected by the programs, especially in poor and minority neighborhoods. In the eyes of some critics, however, the efforts to remedy the problems had transformed the federal government's promise of "maximum feasible participation" in the programs to "maximum feasible misunderstanding," as Daniel Patrick Moynihan put it during his academic days.[2] Critics contended that government programs had grown so large that they worked poorly and that they were unresponsive to the very people they were designed to serve.

On an even broader plane, worries arose that American government was becoming too centered at the national level and, in Washington, was becoming too concentrated in the White House, creating an "imperial presidency."[3] Richard Nixon's Watergate scandal only underlined those concerns.

In struggling with these issues, reformers discovered that the nation had little taste for cutting back on the growth of government spending or for profound structural change. Hardening of Washington's organizational arteries, both in the capital's bureaucracy and especially in the jurisdictions of the members of congressional subcommittees, made it difficult to consider fundamental structural change. Reformers in the 1970s therefore turned to procedural innovation. Instead of cutting back on spending or trying to restructure public agencies, reformers worked to shift government power by changing government procedures. To give state and local governments more power over federal money, first Nixon and then President Gerald Ford worked with Congress to combine existing categorical programs into block grant programs. The new programs broadened the categories in which state and local governments could spend federal cash; they also reduced planning, paperwork, and approval requirements and encouraged subnational governments to spend the money on the problems that they viewed as most important. And then, in a sharp rebuke to Nixon, Congress sought to rebalance spending power by creating a new congressional budget process. Instead of dealing with spending bills one at a time, with appropriations set simply by the program totals approved by Congress, Congress committed itself to setting overall targets for revenue and expenditures and then enforcing those targets on its own committees.

After forty years of virtually uninterrupted accretion of power in Washington and, within Washington, to the executive branch, the reforms of the 1970s—during the Nixon and Ford administrations—marked a turning point. In both political rhetoric and the policymaking process, the early 1970s marked a high point of "slouching toward Washington," as David B. Walker described the evolution of federalism.[4] And as Congress flexed at least some muscle, the period also marked a plateau in the accretion of national power in the White House. State and local governments continued to tussle with Washington over the balance of power, and the rules governing programs like Medicaid and various environmental protection initiatives continued to spark complaints about excessive federal control. For its part, members of Congress regularly bristled at the exercise of presidential power, regardless of which party controlled the White House. But in both the executive and legislative branches, the rise of procedural innovations helped stem the concentration of political power.

When the Reagan administration took office, its officials took a different procedural tack. They began with the ideological conclusion that government, especially in Washington, had gotten too big and too powerful. They recognized that a frontal assault on the New Deal and Great Society welfare state would meet insurmountable opposition, in both the Congress and the nation at large. So they pursued a privatization strategy—trying to turn as much as possible of the government's work over to the private sector, especially through contracting out. The Reagan administration bolstered the strategy with yet another presidential commission, headed by businessman J. Peter Grace. Unlike most previous twentieth-century commissions, which sought to strengthen government's power to manage its programs, the Grace Commission aimed at cutting government and spinning the administration of as many government programs as possible off to the private sector.

Neither Reagan nor his commission had much success on the first front. Federal spending as a share of gross domestic product (the government's contribution to the domestic economy) nudged down slightly, from 22.2 percent in fiscal year 1981 to 21.2 percent in 1989. But government contracting rose substantially. Just how much is difficult to determine, since the federal government does not measure contracting in a clear and consistent way. The anecdotal evidence, however, was huge and substantive, with aggressive contracting out for everything from cafeteria service in federal office buildings to maintenance services on military bases. In a 1999 study, Paul C. Light estimated that the federal government had a "shadow" workforce consisting of 12.7 million full-time–equivalent jobs—compared with the federal government's 1.9 million civilian executive branch employees. For every federal employee, Light determined, there were 6.7 "shadow" employees helping produce the government's goods and services. In some departments, the ratio was even larger. Light calculated that the Department of Energy had thirty-five contractor employees for every federal worker.[5]

In the last half of the twentieth century, government reformers took an approach that was distinctly different from that taken in the first half. To be sure, structural reforms continued, including the creation of the Environmental Protection Agency, the Department of Energy, the Department of Education, and the Department of Veterans Affairs, which were to coordinate programs in their respective realms. But most of the efforts were more cosmetic than substantive. The creation of the Department of Homeland Security in 2002 was more typical of the structural reforms undertaken in the first half of the twentieth century, but such fundamental restructurings have been more the exception than the rule. Likewise, the federal government continued to explore policy innovations, most notably with the establishment of the Medicare and Medicaid programs, which had an enormous reach across all levels and sectors of American government. The most substantial and long-lasting reforms, however, focused on procedural shifts: changing the government's rules and tactics to make government work better and, in the case of the Reagan efforts, to try to make it smaller and cheaper, too.

The Clinton Administration and "Reinventing Government"

Until the Clinton administration launched its "reinventing government" initiative in 1993, there had been no comprehensive strategy to match the "new public management" efforts under way in many other nations. Borrowing the label from a bestseller written by David Osborne, a writer, and Ted Gaebler, a former city manager, the Clinton administration launched its new strategy, which was in many respects more ambitious than many of the new public management strategies.[6] It targeted more nooks and crannies of government than the efforts in other nations had; on the other hand, because of the political conflict it engendered, it focused on changing bureaucrats' behavior rather than transforming fundamental government structures and processes.

Largely because of the efforts of renegade independent candidate H. Ross Perot, the 1992 presidential election campaign generated surprising debate about government's size and performance. Soon after winning the election, President Bill Clinton and his political strategists decided that they needed to develop an initiative to take back the 19 percent of the vote that Perot had won. Clinton committed the administration to reinventing American government—to make government smarter, cheaper, and more effective—and charged Vice President Al Gore with leading the effort. Gore devoted a surprising amount of attention to the job and soon became closely identified with the movement. Americans had proven inveterate reformers during the twentieth century, and reinventing government became the latest and, in many ways, the most ambitious step.[7]

The Gore effort provoked remarkably different responses. The administration hailed reinvention as "creating a government that works better and cost less."[8] Cynics rejected the effort as meaningless, and critics argued that it was dangerous to democracy.[9] Management expert Peter Drucker contended that steps that Gore claimed as radical were trivial ones that in other institutions "would not even be announced, except perhaps on the bulletin board in the hallway." Drucker said that they were the kinds of things "that even a poorly run manufacturer expects supervisors to do on their own—without getting much praise, let alone extra rewards."[10]

Three Phases of Reinvention

Because the Gore-led movement encompassed not one but three different "reinventions" in its first six years, sorting out the claims and complaints is difficult. The initiative evolved throughout the Clinton administration, partly to adjust to what the reinventors learned along the way and even more to respond to lurching political counterpressures.

In phase one, the administration launched the initiative and scored some important early victories. In phase two, Clinton's reinventors scrambled to cope with the challenges of the Republican takeover of Congress after the 1994 midterm elections. Finally, in phase three, the reinventors worked to reinvigorate the initiative and to position Gore for the 2000 presidential election. Those shifts made it difficult to characterize or judge the Clinton administration's reinventing government strategy, but at least they chart the big issues that defined it.

Phase One: "Works Better, Costs Less"

Gore's effort was christened the National Performance Review (NPR). For "new Democrats" such as Clinton and Gore, the launch of the reinventing government campaign was a natural first step toward their vision of a new progressivism. "We must reward the people and ideas that work and get rid of those that don't," proclaimed the Clinton–Gore campaign manifesto, and the March 1993 reinventing government announcement put that plan into play.[11] The administration recruited hundreds of federal employees, formed them into teams, and dispatched them throughout the federal bureaucracy to identify opportunities for decreasing waste and improving management. In September 1993 Gore assembled their proposals into a report in which he presented 384 recommendations that promised to save $108 billion and to reduce the federal workforce by 12 percent within five years.[12]

Although the "Works better, costs less" motto had a clever ring to it, it also presented the reinventors with a dilemma.[13] The "works better" aspect envisioned motivating and empowering employees to do a better job, whereas the "costs less" aspect sought to eliminate unneeded positions and programs. Both inside and outside the White House, reinventors felt heavy pressure to show that the NPR was effective by saving large amounts of money, and one action that could quickly produce substantial savings was to reduce federal employment. The NPR promised to permanently eliminate 252,000 federal employees, and Congress later upped the ante to 272,900. That strategy, however, made it hard to motivate federal employees.

Although downsizing drove the debate, two other initiatives were important in phase one: procurement reform and customer service. In 1994 Congress passed the Federal Acquisition Streamlining Act, which simplified procurement regulations and gave managers more flexibility in buying goods off the shelf. It was the first major reform of government contracting rules in a decade. It made managers' lives easier and saved hundreds of millions of dollars, although the precise size of the savings was hard to estimate. Reformers soon hailed it as one of the most important accomplishments of the reinventing government program. The administration also mandated that all federal agencies develop customer service plans. Although critics argued that citizens were government's owners, not its customers, the customer service initiative undoubtedly launched a major transformation in the way that many federal employees thought about the jobs they did and how they should do them. The initiative encouraged the hundreds of thousands of government employees who had previously focused on helping other government employees get their jobs done to keep broader policy goals in mind. It encouraged them to think about the needs of the citizens for whom government programs had been created rather than focus on each agency's narrow self-interest. Although procurement reform and customer service provided the subtext for phase one, downsizing remained the defining theme.

Phase Two: What Should Government Do?

By the end of 1994 the customer service initiative was under way, Congress had passed procurement reform, and the administration had significantly downsized the federal workforce. Vice President Gore applauded the "heroes of reinvention" who had championed better government and cut red tape. Despite the Clinton administration's efforts, the Republicans—who had taken over both houses of Congress in 1994, for the first time in a generation—proceeded to launch a frenzied bidding war to shrink government radically.

The Republican campaign forced the Clinton administration to shift from phase one's emphasis on how government did its work to what government ought to do. In launching phase two, Gore challenged federal managers to "review everything you do"; he even asked managers to consider the implications if their agency were eliminated.[14] No program was to be taken for granted. Quite simply, Gore wanted to counter the Republicans' effort to challenge what government did and how well it did it.

The Republicans failed to pass most of their proposals. The number of cabinet agencies remained the same, and the threatened massive eradication of federal programs never took place. However, Congress did make substantial budget cuts, and at several points the battle completely closed down the government. In the end the Clinton administration maneuvered its way out of the crisis by outflanking congressional Republicans. Despite the grand rhetorical skirmishes, the battle ended in a draw, with little sorting out of government's functions, reorganizing of its operations, or minimizing of its role.

Phase two provided putty for some of the cracks in the political dikes. With his ongoing "hammer awards" (to celebrate breaking through bureaucratic barriers), Gore recognized the work of agency-level reinventors. The customer service movement bore considerable fruit, especially in the Social Security Administration and the U.S. Customs Service.

Procurement changes helped make the lives of government managers easier and made the federal government a better partner for private contractors. The acquisitions workforce shrank by one-third, and the Air Force Materiel Command claimed a 64 percent reduction in the number of pages in its acquisitions regulations. Assessing cost savings was difficult, although the NPR claimed savings of $12.3 billion in the first four years of the effort.[15] However, budgetary battles eroded much of the enthusiasm generated in phase one and further cemented downsizing and cost saving as the keystones of the NPR.

Phase Three: The Search for Political Relevance

In early 1998 Gore shifted the focus of the NPR again. This time, he changed the program name, National Performance Review, to the National Partnership for Reinventing Government ("the NPR with a silent 'G,'" wags suggested). To signal his reinvention of reinvention, Gore gave the new NPR a new slogan: "America @ Its Best." He used the Internet-style symbol for "at" to emphasize the new role of the information-age government: implementing technologies that could improve its efficiency. He also pledged to continue the quest to deliver better customer service and to attain broad goals such as building a "safe and healthy America," "safe communities," a "strong economy," and the "best-managed government ever." The administration focused most of its reinvention efforts on the thirty-two "high-impact agencies" that dealt most directly with citizens, where failure to reform quickly could further undermine the effort—as in the case of the Internal Revenue Service (IRS). For example, the administration committed the Occupational Safety and Health Administration (OSHA) to reducing worker injuries in the 50,000 most dangerous workplaces by 25 percent before the year 2000; the Food and Drug Administration (FDA) to reducing the drug approval process to one year; and the U.S. Postal Service to delivering 92 percent of local first-class mail overnight.[16]

The goal of phase three, in rhetoric and in reality, was to build an information-age government managed as well as America's best companies. The tactic was to use process reforms to motivate people on the inside and broad policy goals to excite people on the outside.[17] Therein lay the central dilemma of phase three: its inside-government game focused on improving the federal government's performance while its outside-government game promised results that the federal government had little role in producing. Federal control over the economy is indirect at

best, weak in the short term, and always hard to measure. Local governments police the streets, even if they are aided by extra police funded by
federal grants. The health and safety of the nation as a whole is obviously
everyone's first concern, but the forces that shape it are so complex that
assigning responsibility (or blame or credit, for that matter) is difficult
indeed. In seeking political relevance, the reinventors necessarily dis-
tanced phase three of the NPR from its ability to achieve and produce
measurable results.

In phase three the government made promises that it could not directly
fulfill and focused government employees on problems they could not
solve themselves. The gap between megapolitics (especially the broad
political battles between the administration and Congress) and frontline
management (especially the experiments that managers undertook to
improve results) had been a problem during phases one and two. In phase
three, with more expansive promises and even tougher political battles,
the gap threatened to widen even more. Such tensions, in the end, made
it difficult for Gore to capitalize on the effort during his 2000 presidential campaign. The candidate rarely mentioned reinventing government
and, in the end, lost to George W. Bush.

The Impacts of Reinvention

What did the National Performance Review produce? Realists (or, perhaps, cynics) argue that the NPR did not accomplish all that it promised.
Pragmatists argue that the goals of the NPR are part of an endless quest.
The twentieth century alone has seen eleven major government reform
initiatives, from the Keep Commission (1905–09) through the two
Hoover Commissions (1947–49 and 1953–55) to the NPR.[18] Indeed, as
Paul Light has argued, endless "tides of reform" have swept American
politics.[19] Especially in American politics, the impulse for public management reform never ebbs for long.

Works Better?

Energetic administrators throughout the federal government developed
imaginative approaches to improving efficiency. Managers in radiology
departments at Veterans Affairs hospitals developed electronic links that
reduced the need for on-call radiologists. Postal workers in Newton,
Massachusetts, saved $50 million with their "Mover's Guide" and "Wel-
come Kit," which improved service and reduced the Postal Service's costs.

The mandate to develop customer service plans had forced all federal agencies to identify and address the customers that they were in business to serve, and reform had streamlined the government's procurement process. NPR officials claimed that more than 4,000 customer service standards had been implemented in more than 570 government agencies and programs. About 325 "reinvention laboratories" were developing innovative approaches to public service delivery.[20]

However, in many agencies the NPR had little impact. In 1996, more than three years after the launch of the NPR, only 37 percent of federal employees surveyed believed that their organization had made reinvention a top priority. The management improvement goals of the NPR penetrated far less deeply into the Pentagon than in civilian agencies.[21] Morale in many agencies was poor. Only 20 percent of federal workers said that the NPR had brought positive change to government. In agencies where the NPR was a top priority, 59 percent of employees thought productivity had improved; where it was not, only 32 percent thought so. Employees in agencies where the goals of the NPR had been emphasized were three times as likely as employees in agencies where its goals were not emphasized to think that government organizations had made good use of their abilities. Employees also were almost twice as likely to believe that they had been given greater flexibility.[22] The attitudes of employees varied with the priority that top managers had placed on reinvention.

The results of that survey underscore one of the most subtle yet most important failures of the NPR effort: despite Gore's surprising and ongoing enthusiasm for the initiative, the administration failed to enlist many of its own political appointees in the cause. Without strong political leadership from those appointees, many agencies did not connect with the NPR campaign. Did government work better because of the NPR? Procurement reform and customer service were clear victories, but the wide disparity in reform efforts among agencies makes generalized conclusions difficult.

Costs Less?

What about the NPR's claim that government cost less? The Clinton administration claimed that if all of its recommendations had been adopted, the federal budget would have saved $177 billion by fiscal year 1999. Actual savings, the NPR estimated, totaled $112 billion.[23] However, those claims were unaudited—and unauditable.[24] Some were clear and straightforward: federal employment was reduced by just over

300,000 positions—15.5 percent, by November 1997—to fewer than 2 million civilian employees.[25] Others were ambiguous and difficult to measure, such as reforms in procurement, information technology, and administrative processes.

However, no matter how cynical an observer might be, one fact was clear: the NPR did indeed reduce the number of federal government employees to a level lower than at any time since the Kennedy administration. Moreover, that reduction accounted for half of all of the NPR's claimed savings. Even if critics might debate specific savings estimates, the reinventing government initiative unquestionably saved a substantial amount of money—if only from the documented downsizing.

Where did the downsizing occur? Data indicate that most reductions took place among federal civilian defense employees and low-level federal workers. There is little evidence that it targeted middle- and upper-management jobs. Overall, the federal civilian workforce (excluding the U.S. Postal Service) shrank 15.4 percent from January 1993 through April 1998. Civilian defense department employment accounted for a large part of the reduction, largely because of the overall reduction in the nation's defense establishment. The procurement workforce shrank, as did the number of frontline white- and blue-collar support workers. Employment elsewhere in the bureaucracy shrank less, but reductions varied widely across the government.

Downsizing had begun in the Pentagon before the launch of the NPR, and cynics contended that the NPR simply ratified reductions in the Department of Defense civilian workforce that were going to occur anyway. Some critics argued that the NPR had accomplished little because the Pentagon was already in the process of downsizing, defense employment accounted disproportionately for the NPR's workforce reductions, and those reductions accounted for the lion's share of the confirmed NPR savings. In fact, the NPR accelerated the defense department trend, and it also spread the reductions to the civilian agencies. The reductions were real and, for some government employees, extremely painful. Indeed, if the NPR accomplished nothing else, it certainly produced a substantial and sustained reduction in federal employment—almost across the board—in a way never before seen in the federal government.

In federal departments, the impact of the workforce reduction varied widely. Although the overall workforce was reduced by a little more than one-sixth, the Justice Department actually grew 21 percent (largely because of the hiring of new prison guards), and some agencies and departments were reduced only slightly. The Environmental Protection Agency (EPA), for example, shrank 2.2 percent and the Department of Health and Human Services 4.2 percent. Other agencies took much bigger hits: the Department of Housing and Urban Development downsized by 23.1 percent, the Department of Defense by 23.4 percent, the General Services Administration by 30.8 percent, and the Office of Personnel Management (OPM) by 47.4 percent.[26] OPM spun off most of the government's personnel decisions to the agencies, whereas Department of Defense reductions were part of a far larger downsizing of the military. The federal government's downsizing was not one phenomenon but many; the reasons were as varied as the agencies themselves.

The Clinton administration also had committed itself to reducing the federal government's middle management. This part of the strategy mirrored the private sector reforms of the 1980s, in which "delayering" and other tactics to reduce the distance from top managers to frontline workers dominated corporate transformations. The argument, in both cases, was simple. Top-level managers make the key policy decisions; frontline workers deliver the services. However, mid-level managers, the argument went, only pushed paper and contributed to bureaucracy. Reformers believed that minimizing the number of bureaucratic layers and increasing the span of control (the number of employees each manager supervised) would better focus organizations on their work and improve their responsiveness to customers.

Such rhetoric drove the federal government's downsizing; however, the results were very different. The biggest reductions in federal employment came not in the management ranks but in support positions. Workers in general schedule (GS) levels 1–4 (low-level clerical and blue-collar workers) shrank by about half. The number of mid-level clerical workers (GS 5–8) as well as entry- and mid-level professional and technical workers (GS 9–12) decreased. However, the number of managers (GS 13–15) actually increased a bit. Quite simply, the reality did not match the rhetoric.[27]

What accounts for the disparity? Almost all personnel reductions were voluntary. The government made available $25,000 payments, in addition to accrued retirement benefits, for workers who agreed to leave the government. That meant that the fit between the NPR's overall downsizing strategy and its long-term results depended far more on individuals' calculations than on the decisions of the NPR's chiefs. Even more important, the reductions depended on shifts in the federal government's management and policy strategies. Much of the reduction in GS levels 1–4 came through defense downsizing. As military bases closed, the workers most likely to be affected were blue-collar support staff, from mechanics to janitors. Those workers tended to fall near the bottom of the federal government's pay scale, and, for the most part, they moved to employment in the private sector. In addition, the federal government markedly increased its contracting out of services ranging from operating cafeterias in federal buildings to planning for government programs. That strategy was fueled by reductions in the number of GS-5–12 employees who previously might have done that work and by the overall strategy of reducing government employment where possible. More contracting out meant proportionately fewer federal frontline workers (because the front lines were increasing in the private sector under contract) and proportionately more high-level managers (who were charged with negotiating, writing, and overseeing the contracts). Thus much of the NPR's downsizing reflected not so much the "reduce middle management" rhetoric as the shifting tactics of federal program implementation.

Indeed, the decrease in the number of low-level federal workers that occurred while the number of high-level workers remained constant or even increased was part of a longer-term "grade creep." During the past thirty years, the average grade level of federal employees has been inching upward, from about GS-7 in 1960 to more than GS-9 at the turn of the century. Critics occasionally have pointed to grade creep as evidence of the federal government's increasing bureaucracy and self-absorption. Part of the source is undoubtedly the increase in the federal government's layers, especially at top levels of the bureaucracy. Paul Light has concluded that those layers have reduced the federal government's responsiveness and impeded its effectiveness.[28]

Much of the grade creep flows directly from the federal government's changing policy tactics. As federal entitlement, grant, loan, and regulatory programs have increased—and direct service delivery has steadily decreased—the federal workforce has adjusted accordingly.

The more complex question is whether the NPR accelerated that well-established trend. Evidence indicates that the downsizing and changes in administrative tactics that the NPR represented may have further shifted government employment to top-level workers. What is difficult to separate out is the contribution of defense downsizing to the trend. The defense buildup of the 1980s tended to lower the grade level of federal workers, as the Pentagon added clerical staff to process contracts and increased defense workers in the field. Defense downsizing naturally would have reduced that trend and, as it reduced the number of lower-level employees, driven the average grade level back up. Only time will show the NPR's contribution to federal government grade creep. However, in the long run the NPR appears to have modestly accelerated a well-established trend based on the federal government's changing strategies and tactics.

The NPR was most notable for its failure to grapple with these long-run trends. Its top officials were preaching the virtues of reducing middle management just as the private sector was rediscovering the importance of middle managers as "high-impact players."[29] The NPR failed to deal with the layering of government and especially with the 3,000 political appointees who encrusted the top of the federal bureaucracy, for the obvious political reasons. That oversight, coupled with the NPR's failure to enlist those appointees aggressively in its cause, marked a major shortcoming of the program. It also made it harder for the NPR to deliver on its promise to downsize middle-level management en route to better customer service. It is hard to reduce the distance from top managers to the shop floor when the shop floor—those who actually deliver the government's goods and services—increasingly lies outside the government.

Although the NPR unquestionably decreased costs, especially through procurement reform and reduction of the number of government employees, assessing which of the recommendations produced which savings is a virtually impossible task for two reasons: because it usually was difficult to predict what costs would have been without the NPR and because the government's cost accounting systems frequently make such analyses impossible.

The one certain conclusion is that the federal civilian workforce was smaller than it would have been without the NPR and that the reduction has saved substantial salary and benefit costs, over both the short and long term. It also is likely that the grade creep in the permanent work force accelerated. Other savings (for example, in areas such as procurement reform) are real but more difficult to assess because what the government's costs would have been absent the reforms is unknown. Finally, many estimated savings are based more on hopes than on actual measures of dollars saved. Did the NPR produce real savings? Yes, specifically in downsizing the federal work force and in streamlining procurement.

The Fruits of Reinvention

Whatever its economic and programmatic impact, the NPR had one clear political result: it inescapably connected Vice President Al Gore, who tirelessly led the effort, with management reform. In fact, many political observers noted Gore's surprisingly consistent and energetic pursuit of reinvention, despite its obvious lack of political sex appeal and the many other demands on his time as one of the Clinton administration's few proven "go-to" officials. As the vice president geared up his 2000 presidential campaign, the NPR had become part of his identity, along with environmental policy and high-tech initiatives. Gore sensed the importance of the NPR but became entrapped in its political paradox. Bruising battles over health care reform, Social Security, and Medicare showed how little stomach Americans had for major policy initiatives— and how much they wanted a government that worked better.

The Clinton administration promised a government that was closer to the people (smaller, more effective, with better customer service), but the effort—clearly designed for its potential to lure Perot voters and define a "new Democrat" approach to governance in 1993—barely registered on the political radar screen. It often was buried under the avalanche of stories about political fundraising and the Whitewater scandal. Reports of abuse of taxpayers by the IRS, from armed agents bursting into taxpayers' homes to complaints about indecipherable tax instructions, further undermined the effort. The IRS scandals were precisely the kind of government problems that the NPR was designed to root out. They put Gore and the NPR in a difficult situation. The NPR, designed as a signature Clinton administration initiative, had failed to ignite popular enthusiasm. Focused on improving government performance, it had failed to insulate the administration from major embarrassment. Conceived as an administrative strategy to increase political support, reinvention had significant but uneven administrative results and relatively little political impact.

Nevertheless, the federal government's productivity challenge—getting more government service for less taxpayer money—made reinvention inescapable and continued reform inevitable. In the process, the reinventors worked to devise new strategies to provide extra control over the government's activities.

The Government Performance and Results Act

Passed in 1993, the Government Performance and Results Act (GPRA) required all federal agencies to develop strategic plans for their activities and establish indicators for measuring outcomes by March 2000. Previous federal reformers had launched a parade of similar, if less ambitious, efforts: Defense Secretary Robert McNamara's only partly fulfilled promise in the 1960s to bring a planning, programming, and budgeting system to the Pentagon; Richard Nixon's goal- and objective-based system, management by objectives (MBO); Jimmy Carter's effort to promote zero-based budgeting (ZBB); and various organizational behavior reforms in the 1980s through total quality management (TQM). The alphabet of reforms—PPB begot MBO, which begot ZBB, which begot TQM—led to GPRA. Cynics quickly predicted that the ambitious new search for federal goals and outcomes soon would lead to the employment of many more consultants and yet another acronym to replace a failed strategy. Some government managers, skeptical of the constant parade of reforms, concluded that they could safely burrow in and allow this new reform to pass them by.

But GPRA was different from previous efforts in two significant ways. First, Congress invested itself directly in GPRA by passing it into law. Second, both Congress and the Clinton administration quickly found political value in the legislation. In 1997 House Majority Leader Dick Armey discovered that GPRA could serve as a device for bringing executive branch officials before congressional committees to answer for their programs. His GPRA "report cards" attracted media attention and embarrassed many senior federal managers. The Office of Management and Budget (OMB), for its part, began relying on GPRA to shape agencies' activities. As entitlements and other uncontrolled spending took up a steadily rising share of the federal budget, OMB officials were eager for a tool that improved their control of the operations of federal agencies. These political questions produced big political squabbles, but the GPRA got a bigger spotlight than its predecessors ever enjoyed. Third, some agencies, including EPA, the National Aeronautics and Space Administration (NASA), the IRS, and the Department of Defense, began using the GPRA process to improve internal management. Even though the applications have been rudimentary, GPRA will achieve greater staying power to the degree that it proves useful to managers in improving the way that they manage their agencies. Indeed, the principal weakness of its predecessors was the failure of the reform tools to become integrated with internal management—and external political—processes.

Information Technology

Vice President Gore became at least as well-known for his interest in the Internet and technology as for his interest in reinventing government. Indeed, for the Clinton reinventors, the NPR and information technology were inextricable. They saw information technology as the central nervous system of the government of the future: a way to make tax filing easier, to integrate services more fully, to improve customer service. In fact, when the administration launched phase three of the NPR in the spring of 1998, the information-based "office of the future" was one of its signature pieces.

Throughout 1999 the NPR's information technology leadership was more rhetorical than real, primarily because the NPR had a tiny staff and because the structure of the federal government is extraordinarily complex. However, the reformers' instinct to focus on information technology had great potential. The less hierarchy shapes public management, the more managers need tools to cross bureaucratic boundaries and link interdependent operations. Moreover, reformers everywhere have sought to improve the integration of public services—for example, to bring together the job training, day care, transportation, and job placement services on which welfare reform depends. Service integration means thinking spatially instead of functionally—and from the bottom up, about how programs come together to affect service recipients, instead of from the top down, as top managers and policymakers create and shape individual programs.[30]

Devolution

While Gore worked on reinventing the federal government, a subtle revolution was quietly transforming American management. The federal government increasingly devolved administrative responsibilities and policy-shaping decisionmaking to the states. Americans had invented modern federalism in the eighteenth century, and the states always have had substantial responsibility for many domestic programs. However, in the twentieth century the federal government expanded the scope of domestic policy and imposed new restrictions on the states in managing them. As the federal government struggled to reinvent its own operations, it passed more responsibility back to the states.

For example, the federal government proudly "ended welfare as we know it" by giving the states responsibility for getting welfare recipients off the dole and into productive jobs. EPA delegated more authority to the states in devising strategies for reaching pollution reduction goals. The states experimented with new managed care plans for their Medicaid recipients and devised innovative performance management systems. Contracting out by local governments to for-profit and nonprofit organizations increased substantially.[31] Meanwhile, the states vastly expanded their reliance on private and nonprofit contractors in running programs ranging from welfare to prison operations and management as they struggled to make the programs cheaper and more effective.

The evidence from America's states and cities supports the conclusion that the connection between administrative reform and political success has been tight at the state and local levels. A new generation of pragmatists has risen in many state capitals and city halls. In the nation's best-run states and cities, it is hard to find a distinctly Republican or Democratic theme that shapes the approach to policy problems. From Republican Mayor Stephen Goldsmith's massive privatization of Indianapolis public services to Democratic Mayor Michael White's transformation of Cleveland, a new generation of state and local officials has defined success by getting things done. Such efforts do not mean that the political parties have evaporated or that former Mayor Rudolph Giuliani did not trumpet his Republicanism as the reason for the reduction in New York City's crime. However, it does mean that state and local elected officials—especially the most successful ones—have made getting results their number-one priority. Voters, in turn, have looked at results more than party in casting their ballots. The triumph of pragmatism over partisanship has produced widely heralded successes (cheaper, more effective, more responsive government) as well as clear political payoffs, because voters elect leaders with demonstrated track records.

One of the great ironies of the effort to reinvent and shrink the federal government is that it promoted the transfer of more programs to the states. Indeed, American devolution is a triumph of pragmatism, but it also is an often bewildering way of sharing administrative power. That devolution clearly has improved the responsiveness of American government, but it has blurred the lines of responsibility and made it harder to determine who is accountable for which results—especially when compared with reforms in other nations, which sought to set sharp policy goals and then establish clear responsibility for outcomes. The American reforms have blurred the process of setting and achieving goals. Management reform in the U.S. government has a unique style, very different from efforts elsewhere in the world.

Reinvention's Lessons

Even though the Clinton administration's reinventing government initiative encountered serious problems, it showed genuine accomplishment.

It saved a significant amount of money, brought substantial managerial reforms (especially in customer service and procurement processes), and promoted a more performance-based discussion on the functions of government. Vice President Gore so strongly championed the campaign that Republicans determined to tar him with its shortcomings.

However, the shortcomings of the NPR are as instructive as its successes. President Clinton's bold proclamation about the end of "big government" missed the far more important if much more subtle transformation in the way government works in the United States. The NPR demonstrated, in both its achievements and its failures, that the federal government is no longer organized to do the job that law and the Constitution charge it to do. The federal government particularly has not built the capacity required to effectively manage a government increasingly operated through proxies. Both Democrats and Republicans have been politically burned on megapolicy initiatives, and neither side has shown much stomach for further adventures.

For these reasons the management agenda is all the more important. They also underline a critical point: that management reform is at least as much about politics and governance as it is about management. Beyond this point is an even subtler one: policy initiatives have important management implications that can be ignored only at great political peril.

The Bush Management Agenda

It was hardly surprising that one of the George W. Bush administration's first steps was to close down the Clinton reinventing government office and the program it ran. Having beaten the champion of the effort, the new administration was not about to allow any vestiges to survive. But following the privatization initiatives in the Reagan administration and the Clinton reinventing government campaign, management reform had become firmly established at the top levels of American government. Bush came into office with his own, different plan. Unlike the massive Clinton effort, with its hundreds of initiatives scattered throughout government and managed from a small office up 17th Street from the White House, Bush developed an effort tightly focused on results and managed from the Office of Management and Budget. In his management plan, Bush said:

> Government likes to begin things—to declare grand new programs
> and causes and national objectives. But good beginnings are not the

measure of success. What matters in the end is completion. Performance. Results. Not just making promises, but making good on promises. In my Administration, that will be the standard from the farthest regional office of government to the highest office of the land.[32]

The Bush five-point management agenda began with attention to the strategic management of human capital. It sought to expand significantly the government's contracting out of services, and it pledged improved financial management. It expanded the federal government's "e-government" initiatives. Finally, and most important, it sought to measure the performance of federal programs and to integrate performance information into budget decisions.

The effort to integrate performance with the budget was a massive step. Over a five-year period, the Bush administration ordered the managers of all federal programs to define strategic goals and to devise performance measures for assessing their achievement of those goals. The federal government had long sought to link budgeting with performance, especially with the famous reforms—including the Planning Programming Budgeting System, or PPBS for short—introduced by Robert McNamara into the Pentagon. Bush's effort marked the broadest and most aggressive performance measurement effort in the nation's history. Congress in 1993 had already mandated that federal agencies measure the performance of their programs, so there was little room for backsliding.

Of course, determining what to do with the performance numbers proved a major challenge. Did a low grade suggest problems that more money could solve? Or would more money simply serve to fund more of what had already been shown not to work? Cynics sometimes suggested that the Bush performance measurement system did little more than provide a rationalization for ideological decisions that the administration had already made. But despite the debate, it is clear that by tying the performance measures to budgets and by backing them up with OMB's muscle, the Bush administration produced more movement on performance measurement than the federal government had previously seen.

A keystone of the effort was a "traffic light" scoreboard for each federal department, with red lights for unsatisfactory performance, yellow for mixed results, and green for success. OMB proved a tough grader. After almost two years, federal agencies earned just four green lights of a total of 130. Two-thirds of the grades were red lights. OMB launched a major initiative to try to help more agencies "get to green," and the capital region's vast network of contractors sprang to work helping agency managers improve their performance scores.[33] The traffic-light system proved a marvelously simple and powerful tool for attracting attention to the president's management agenda, for creating lively news stories for the press, and for making it difficult for top department mangers to escape the pressure to improve results.

Unlike with the Clinton effort, there were few simple "costs less" targets like downsizing. However, the traffic-light system coupled with a limited agenda created a focus on the "works better" targets, and Bush budget officials used the performance scores to indicate budget cuts. Critics of the Bush system suspected that it had been constructed to provide analytical justification for cuts the administration wanted to make on ideological grounds. But virtually everyone agreed that moving to a system that was more focused on measuring results and integrating that system with OMB's budget process were both big steps forward.

The ultimate test of the Bush management agenda will depend on its staying power. But it did make several important points. A strategy for government reform has become increasingly central to the presidency. Focused management strategies that are integrated with the budgetary process and supervised through top-level agencies like OMB are more likely to get sustained attention from top government officials.

Finally, getting long-term results depends ultimately on getting Congress to pay attention to management issues—something with which the Clinton and Bush administrations both struggled. Management—the focus on results instead of the creation of policy—simply did not engage many members of Congress. That meant that agency officials constantly faced cross-pressures from Congress on the matters of traditional concern: how money was distributed, how program problems created opportunities for attracting the press to oversight hearings, and how they could intervene in agency activities to help constituents. For presidential reformers, that meant a constant struggle to get and keep the focus of agency officials on the reform agenda.

Sizing Up the Reforms

The reform movements in the Westminster nations and in the United States are striking in comparison (see table 3-1). They are similar in one respect: leaders of both nations committed themselves to aggressive

Table 3-1. *Public Management Reforms:*
Westminster Nations and the United States

	Westminster reforms	American reforms
Model	New economics	Business process improvement
Focus of reform	Transformation of structure	Reform of operations
Goals	Precise	Fuzzy
Role of leadership	Relatively strong	Relatively weak
Role of legislature	Relatively strong	Relatively weak
Results measured	Outputs	Outcomes
Accountability	Managerial, through contracts	Political, through existing systems
Risks	High stakes	Low stakes

reforms and, once the reforms were launched, it was impossible to turn back. However, there also were basic differences in the initial strategy. The Westminster reforms began as fundamental, top-down changes, hardwired into the nation's administrative systems. The American reforms, in contrast, tended to be broader but more organic.

We will turn later to broader assessments of the effectiveness of these efforts. For now, three points are important. One is that the global public management revolution encompasses wide variation in strategies and tactics. The second point, perhaps surprisingly, is that over time reforms have tended toward convergence, characterized by efforts to strengthen the coordination among government programs; strategies to enhance government control over public programs, especially through measurement of outcomes; and efforts to enhance public capacity to deliver results. The final and perhaps most fundamental point is that public management reform has become an intrinsic part of governance in the twenty-first century. When new governments take office, the question increasingly is not whether they will continue reform but rather what shape it will take.

CHAPTER FOUR

Strategies and Tactics

The global government reform movement has focused on two problems. One problem is policy, which has its roots in politics: What should government do? How much should it do? Can—or should—government be smaller? The policy questions revolve around values, and their resolution depends on the political process. The other problem is administration, which seeks to improve efficiency and effectiveness: How can government do what it does better? Can it do more with less and, in the process, improve citizens' satisfaction? Resolving the administrative questions depends on improving the management process—especially the traditional bureaucratic exercise of authority.

The global reform debate suggests several different answers to these questions. One New Zealander is fond of pointing out that his mother, when asked her opinion of the government's administrative reforms there, observed that it still took six months to get a gallbladder operation. Citizens, and many elected officials, often fail to distinguish between deciding what to do and determining how to do it better. Of course, often there is no practical distinction between such political and administrative issues. Government is what government does. Government reform hinges on deciding whether the policy or the management processes—or both—must be changed to improve what government does.

Global administrative reform tactics share a common approach: they try to remedy the pathologies of a traditional hierarchical and authority-driven bureaucracy. In many ways bureaucracy has proven itself a noble invention. In both the private and public sectors, it has allowed people to coordinate complex activities in efficient ways. However, its critics have contended that bureaucracy—especially public bureaucracy—also has produced a host of problems. Bureaucracies can become locked into "iron triangles" and tight "issue networks," in which interest groups and narrow legislative pressures can distort administration. According to the critics, bureaucracies produce miles of red tape.[1] They can become inflexible and rude and consumed by incentives to maximize their own power at the expense of public goals.[2] The complaints about bureaucracy have spread quickly and globally, to that point that "bureaucracy" is a dirty word the world over.

As a central part of their efforts, reformers have sought to transform bureaucracy and the incentives that drive it. The Australians, for example, have viewed bureaucrats as good people trapped in bad systems and have worked to sweep away impediments in order to "let the managers manage." The New Zealanders, by contrast, have viewed bureaucrats as utility maximizers. They have worked to transform the incentives of bureaucrats in order to "make the managers manage."[3] Whatever the approach, the global reform movement has built on a singular effort to transform public bureaucracy.

Herein lies the central dilemma for reformers. Despite its pathologies, bureaucracy is an essential tool of modern government. How can its essential missions be preserved while transforming its behavior? What does government need to do to support the effort?

Reform: Governance and Management

One lesson from the assessment of management reform strategies comes through clearly: the strategies are as much about politics as administration. Indeed, basic governance issues shape the management options. In addition, however, fundamental and common management problems shape the reform strategies.

Governance

The Westminster and American reforms represent the basic models of reform, and the primary characteristics of each shape the choices that reformers can make. In the global management reform movement, the basic strategies have been shaped partly by scale (the extent to which governments have attempted to reshape fundamentally their package of services) and partly by the degree of difficulty of reform (how hard it is to build consensus within a nation's governance system about that package of services). The management reform movement is about government administration—its structures, tools, and processes. However, administration is inextricably linked to governance, and both are rooted in politics. The first generation of reforms teaches an important lesson: management reform strategies must fit into a nation's governance system—and they must be supported by the political system if they are to succeed.

The American reforms rank among the most sweeping. Reinventing government sought to transform the entire U.S. federal government in a very short time—to focus government on its customers, improve its effectiveness, and decrease its costs. GPRA catapulted the U.S. federal government past fifteen years of Westminster experimentation with output measures to a quick, aggressive move into outcome assessment. However, despite contentious debates about what government ought to do, officials from both parties found the question too hot to handle. Six years of reinvention left the federal government about the same size in scope and scale. It had fewer employees, but it also had devolved many responsibilities to state and local governments and to private and nonprofit contractors, who did much of the federal government's work.[4] In the end the NPR sought to make the existing government work better and cost less. The complexity of American government—especially its separation of powers and the divided parties within it—makes it impossible to achieve consensus on what government ought to do, leaving the Clinton administration's reinventors to focus on administrative remedies that avoided basic policy choices.

The Westminster reformers, by contrast, have relied heavily on privatization and other market-type mechanisms, focusing intently on outputs but only modestly on traditional bureaucratic reorganization. The United States privatized little—the federal government had few state-owned enterprises such as telephone companies and airlines to sell off— so it relied more on public-private partnerships and contracting. Its separation-of-powers system encouraged substantial decentralization to lower levels of the bureaucracy in issues ranging from personnel policy to customer service. Meanwhile its federal system led to more devolution to states in areas ranging from welfare reform to environmental policy. The Nordic countries presented a hybrid approach, relying modestly on market mechanisms and much more on reorganization and budgetary reforms. But the American and Westminster nations defined the core reform strategies.

Those basic strategies varied not only by kind of government and degree of change in the government's role but also—subtly but significantly—by the tactics that the nations used. The tactics of each were partly the product of the options that its governance system permitted and encouraged and partly the product of what each sought to accomplish. They also were the products of substantial cross-fertilization. Indeed, one of the most significant features of the global revolution in public management is the spread of reform ideas. Reformers often have been tempted to pluck ideas out of context—for example, from New Zealand's contract-based output system or American welfare reform—without assessing their link with the governance system that created them. One of the most important lessons of management reform is that its strategies must fit within and have the support of the governance system in which they are applied.

Management

In most countries the management reform movement has sought to root out traditional bureaucracy and the pathologies that reformers believe flow from it. They have tried to root out authority-driven hierarchies and replace them with systems that are both more competitive (driven by market strategies) and more responsive (driven by stronger attention to citizens as customers). That approach has brought three fundamental issues to the surface.

First, reform strategies do not manage themselves. They require energetic management by highly skilled public managers. Few of the reforms have been purely market driven. Privatization, for example, involves shifting public programs to the private market, but after state-owned enterprises (telephone and other utilities, airlines, postal services) are sold off, government is left with the job of managing what remains. Experience demonstrates quite clearly that outsourcing and other such tactics, customer service, and information technology do not—and cannot—manage themselves. Indeed, they require aggressive and thoughtful oversight.

Second, that oversight requires a capacity that is substantially different from that provided by traditional government tools managed through traditional bureaucracies.[5] Contracts, vouchers, tax incentives, loan programs, and other indirect tools of government differ from direct service delivery through a bureaucracy in two ways:

—*Although government might purchase the service, it does not directly provide it.* Rather, proxies (in the private or nonprofit sectors or in other levels of government) produce the service instead. In the United States, for example, nearly ninety cents of every federal dollar is spent through entitlement programs and proxies—individuals, state and local governments, and private and nonprofit contractors who manage programs on behalf of the federal government. How well these programs work depends on how well the government's proxies manage the programs on the government's behalf.

—*Only a very small number of the programs funded by the federal budget even remotely match the traditional hierarchical, authority-based governance model.* Government managers operate in bureaucracies, organized hierarchically and controlled by authority, to manage tools that increasingly operate by neither hierarchy nor authority. This is not a purely American phenomenon. The Paris-based Organization for Economic Cooperation and Development (OECD) has invested substantial energy in understanding forms of "alternative service delivery."[6]

Third, the global reform movement seeks to strengthen government's ability to develop coordinated responses to problems that stretch beyond the boundaries of individual bureaucracies. American reinventors sought to provide "one-stop shopping,"[7] whereas the Canadian government explored "citizen-centered program delivery."[8] A 1999 British government white paper committed the government to "joined-up government"—one-stop shops to improve the coordination of government services. The government created new offices and also expanded "virtual" coordination through telephone and Internet information services. In fact, the British government experimented with organizing services around major life events—births, start of school, marriage, death—with government organizations joining together to make those transitions easier.[9] The Scottish government, with powers newly devolved from London, considered "the possible Scot," a strategy for joined-up government that pulled together related health care services.[10]

Reform Tactics: Transforming the Bureaucracy

Bureaucracy's greatest strength lies in coordinating complex operations. However, coordination in the twenty-first century raises a host of new problems, and no bureaucracy can completely encompass, manage, or control any problem that really matters.

Harold Seidman has pointed out that coordination is the "philosopher's stone" of public management. Medieval alchemists believed that if they could find the magic stone, they would find the answers to human problems. Coordination, Seidman argues, has the same appeal for managers and reformers: "If only we can find the right formula for coordination," he wrote, "we can reconcile the irreconcilable, harmonize competing and wholly divergent interests, overcome irrationalities in our government structures, and make hard policy choices to which no one will disagree."[11] Coordination becomes the answer to government's problems; lack of coordination becomes the diagnosis of its failures.

Administration, in both public and private life, is a search for social coordination. It is how leaders pull together widely disparate resources—money, people, expertise, and technology—to get complex tasks done. The implementation of public programs is an intricate dance, whether it is the dispatch of highly trained firefighters to the scene of a blaze or the high-tech ballet in which airplanes fly safely under the direction of air traffic controllers. The global management reform movement is partly about better fitting government programs to citizens' wants, but it also is about building new tools to improve the coordination among government programs.

Budgeting and Accounting

The New Zealand reforms laid the foundation for changes in budgeting and accounting tactics. Its output-driven accrual accounting system provided the basis for reforms in many other nations, especially the Westminster countries. The Nordic countries joined with New Zealand in implementing top-down, fiscally driven budget policies in which the government set broad policy targets and set agency budgets accordingly. Although most other countries did not follow their lead in top-to-bottom reform, some nations substantially increased managers' flexibility in deciding how to meet their targets. In Canada's Expenditure Management System, for example, managers fund new initiatives by reallocating their existing budgets.[12] "Portfolio budgeting" in Australia and the Nordic countries gives managers discretion in how to meet mandated savings targets. In Australia, Denmark, and Sweden, managers enjoy "efficiency dividends": their departments are allowed to keep some of the savings they produce.[13]

Accrual accounting, especially in the Westminster countries, has been an important tool in making government more transparent. Reformers have tried to force government officials to confront the full cost of their decisions as they make them, rather than rely on short-term accounting to shift the costs of present decisions to future years. However, most other nations, including the United States, have stayed with cash-based accounting systems, in which each year's budget is a snapshot of the balance between income and expenses.

In most nations, reformers have looked to budgeting and accounting systems as the very foundation of their efforts. Money provides the most crucial input for most government programs, tracking the money provides the most useful indicator of activity, and reshaping the flow of money provides perhaps the most useful incentive for changing managers' behavior. Hence budgeting and financial management are the bedrock on which most other reforms have been built.

Performance Management

Reformers have transformed performance measurement into performance management by linking the assessment process with management of government strategies and tactics. New Zealand's agency-based contracts, which tie together the government's goals, the agency's budget, and program outputs, are the prototype, but other governments have imitated that approach. The United Kingdom has used a similar approach, and the United States has moved aggressively toward coupling strategic plans with outcomes.

Many governments have gone beyond program performance measurement to employee assessment, setting up pay-for-performance systems for government managers. These systems have spread to Australia, Ireland, the United Kingdom, the United States, and Denmark. However, an OECD survey of government workers in five nations found that performance-driven pay was a relatively weak motivator. In fact, it ranked last of fourteen different factors in the survey. The report concluded that independence on the job, a sense of accomplishment, and having challenging work were far more important motivators.[14] Managers worried that they did not fully understand the criteria by which they were being judged and that the pay available for performance often did not match their performance awards. In general, managers did not object to the concept of performance-driven pay, but they did not believe that awards were distributed fairly or predictably.[15] Other studies have produced remarkably uniform conclusions.[16]

The managerialist movement, founded in economic theories of bureaucracy that presume that incentives motivate performance, had suggested that performance-driven pay would reshape the behavior of government managers. However, in practice the performance-driven pay systems have tended not to be funded or implemented predictably. Senior government managers in particular have paid far more attention to the challenges that their job offers. Put differently, public managers around the world have indeed been strongly motivated by incentives, but the incentives have had more to do with their jobs than with often sporadic performance-driven pay systems. The OECD study concluded that there were serious questions about "whether [performance-related pay] awards of any form or size will ever have sufficient value for public sector managers" to make the tactic effective.[17]

The New Zealand and U.K. experience proved the value of measuring the outputs of public programs. Indeed, such performance management systems became the keystone of reform efforts around the world. In the United States, discussion began on using performance measures to find balance among competing customer expectations. This system has led to "families" of performance measures that allow managers to assess the impact of their programs on different groups.[18] However, extension of the tactic—both from outputs to outcomes and from programs to managers—has proved troublesome. Only more experience will tell whether the problems stem from a lack of experience or from inherent limitations of the tools.

Contracting

Reformers have relied extensively on expanding partnerships with nongovernmental organizations—contractors in the private and nonprofit sectors. In nations with federal systems—especially Australia, Canada, and the United States—reformers also have substantially expanded partnerships between the national and state governments. The reasons are both political and administrative. Nations everywhere have faced strong citizen demands to shrink the size of the state. Such partnerships provide ways of getting government's work done without government itself having to do it. Moreover, partnerships provide governments with more flexibility for tackling tough management chores. Governments often can hire and fire partners far more easily than they can shift the number of government workers, and they often can acquire much-needed skills more easily through partnerships than by recruiting and training their own workers.

Perhaps most important, much of the contracting movement has been driven by the assumption that government is inherently inefficient and that by relying more on nongovernmental contractors, government can reduce its costs and improve its results. That assumption is based partly on a powerful ideological belief on the right, often quite untested by evidence, about the superiority of the private sector. More subtly, some of it flows from the belief that government's role is primarily to define goals and that it does not necessarily have to produce services itself. The former argument has dominated debate in the United States, where the push for privatization, contracting, and other forms of shifting power from government to the private sector has come largely from conservative circles.[19] The latter argument, by contrast, dominated thinking in the Westminster countries, especially New Zealand.

This disparity in the underlying philosophy has led to very different public-private partnerships around the world. In the United States, the presumed superiority of the private sector has led some reformers, especially at the state and local level, to contract out everything possible in the belief that simply shifting administration to contractors would improve efficiency naturally. That presumed superiority has led to relatively less concern about how best to structure and manage partnerships; simply creating them, some reformers assumed, would lead to better results. In New Zealand, a different kind of antibureaucratic ideology drove the debate. Reformers assumed that the self-interested incentives offered to bureaucrats crippled their performance and that a contract-based system between purchasers of government services (the government and its cabinet) and their providers (in the bureaucracy or in nongovernmental partnerships) would prevent those difficulties. This assumption increased attention on the need to manage contracts well, because the principal–agent economic theory that supported the movement also explored the pathologies of contracts—especially transaction costs such as information and supervision problems—extensively. Moreover, there was no built-in bias toward contracting out; a job was to be done by whoever could do it best.

The evidence for these theories remains rather thin; far more decisions have been based on ideology than on research. Nevertheless, a 1998 OECD survey of experiences in Australia, Denmark, Iceland, Sweden, the United Kingdom, and the United States showed that savings from contracting out ranged from 5 to 50 percent; typical savings reported in the study were 20 percent.[20] However, the "level playing field" argument always intrudes on these measures: Do contractors provide the same level of service that government workers provide? Do they maintain the same focus on broad social values, such as fairness and equality? Do they bid low at the beginning to get the contract and then raise prices later? Although the OECD report acknowledged that "there is some debate whether levels of quality of service were always maintained while these savings were being achieved," it nevertheless concluded that "what does seem clear is that effectively implemented contracting out can lead to productivity improvements."[21]

The key issue, at least in the Australian and in some aspects of the American experience, is the existence of real competition—what the Australians call contestability. According to one OECD study, it is not so much the public or private nature of an activity that determines its efficiency and effectiveness as "the *prospect* of competition." The study concluded, "Contestability in the public service does not necessarily imply transfer or provision of services to the private sector. In numerous instances [in Australia], services that were once provided by the Federal public service are now being delivered by a different arm or level of government. Indeed, many services continue to be delivered by the same provider but in a better manner because of the effect of contestability."[22]

The Australian study found that contestability resulted in substantial savings. The Defence Commercial Support Program, for example, achieved recurring annual savings of AUS$100 million, and Australia Post, the nation's postal service, increased annual productivity growth from 1 percent in 1990 to 6.8 percent in 1993–94. Contestability also improved service and product quality, transparency, and accountability.[23]

Similarly, in the United States competition between public and private suppliers of public services has underscored the value of competition. Since 1979 Phoenix has put up for bid fifty-six different service contracts in thirteen different functional areas, ranging from data entry and fuel distribution to street sweeping and senior citizen housing management. In thirty-four cases, private contractors submitted the low bids. However, in twenty-two competitions, city workers won the work, outcompeting private bidders. In the process, the city saved $27 million.[24] In Indianapolis local officials moved aggressively to a process they called "contracting in."[25] The competitive process, not who won the competition, proved to be the source of efficiency gains.

The key to making such processes work is the government's capacity to write and manage contracts effectively. Government, in short, must become a smart buyer; it must clearly specify what it wants to buy, run a fair and competitive procurement process, and carefully assess the quality of what it buys.[26] The need for effective contract management has led to the development of new management tools, from information technology and performance measurement to human resources and leadership.[27]

In the United States the NPR's procurement reforms played a major role in reinvention, and Vice President Al Gore emphasized the role of exercising common sense in making purchases. The U.S. Navy, for example, had procurement regulations that called for "ruggedized" telephones on board its ships. These devices, which were guaranteed to continue working even if the ship sank, cost $450 per unit. However, on the new aircraft carrier *U.S.S. John C. Stennis*, procurement officers installed off-the-shelf phones that cost $30 each. Laughing, Gore admitted that "if the ship sinks and is refloated, this phone will not work." He added, "If you do the calculation, you would actually have to sink and refloat the ship fifteen times in order to enjoy the cost savings from the ruggedized phone. So, we've decided to just buy these phones at commercial outlets instead of the specialized models. And you know, if your ship is sinking and being refloated fifteen times, you're going to be worried about other things than telephone calls anyway."[28]

Customer Service

The concept of improving government's service to citizens—and using that strategy to transform bureaucracy—has been one of the most robust features of reform. It is a two-part effort. To improve citizens' trust in and support for government, public officials have worked to make government services more friendly, convenient, and seamless. Instead of making citizens accommodate government—its schedules and its way of doing business—officials have tried to accommodate citizens.

An NPR report argued, "We have to restore confidence that we can all work effectively together through self-government. And the government has to build confidence just like Ford—or any good company—does. With each and every customer." Government "was getting away from us," the report continued. "It was marching to different drummers—special interests, Washington professionals, well-meaning people with good intentions—on a path that seemed to be headed away from the taxpaying customers of government." By developing customer service strategies that focus on what people want, the report concluded, government could map out "a dramatic change of direction, a big U-turn, to head government back to the people."[29] Customer service, the NPR believed, would both help restore confidence in government and provide a powerful engine for changing how government did its job. In fact, the Social Security Administration surprised the business world when an independent survey found that the agency had the country's best toll-free telephone service.[30]

The movement toward better customer service has been very broad. In addition to the United Kingdom, with its "citizens' charters," Belgium, France, and Portugal have set standards for customer service. In Australia, France, and Germany, citizens can receive written explanations of government decisions that affect them.[31] Many governments, both national and local, have developed strategies to make service delivery more seamless for citizens. Italy, for example, has established a one-stop shop for businesses wherein authorization can be provided for the location and start-up of a new plant or the expansion of an existing one.[32] The French government has even used the services of a "qualitician," a quality control expert, to expand customer service concepts.[33] In South Africa, tactics to increase the transparency of government and improve customer service were central to the government's efforts to uproot apartheid. The national *Bitupili* ("people first") program established outcome measures, public reporting systems, and complaint procedures.[34]

The American customer service movement is one of the most robust (in terms of experiments launched) and least developed (in terms of knowledge and concepts).[35] Part of the problem, as NPR's critics pointed out, is that citizens are "owners" of government as well as service recipients.[36] Moreover, many government services do not share the basic private sector customer–provider relationship. Government usually has no choice about whether to provide key services, and citizens often have no choice about whether to go to government for those services. It is the element of choice that drives customer service in the private sector: companies can decide which products to build and market, and customers can decide which products they prefer to buy—if indeed they choose to purchase any products at all. Thus companies have strong incentives to build and service products that bring them the greatest profit, and customers have strong incentives to patronize companies that provide the greatest satisfaction. Citizens typically cannot choose which fire department or social security agency to patronize, and the fire department cannot choose to go into the social security business. Lack of choice dramatically limits the options on both sides of the government service delivery system and thus reduces critical incentives for efficient and effective delivery.

In government, therefore, customer service has become more a symbol—broad goals without specific processes. It is difficult to argue with the notion that government ought to do whatever it can do to make its services more responsive and to make citizen–government interactions less difficult. For example, government can accommodate citizens' work schedules by making the hours and locations of driver's license bureaus more flexible. Tax forms and instructions can be designed to be easier to understand. However, the customer service movement runs headlong into the fact that neither side typically has a choice in whether to have a relationship in the first place, especially for core government services. And while citizens expect quick, friendly, and convenient government services, they may not be happy about paying for them—especially when the services benefit someone else.

The private sector has not solved this dilemma either. The corporate landscape is littered with spectacular marketing failures, from the Edsel to "new Coke." Many of the core methods and problems in the government and the private sector are remarkably uniform: identifying the customer, determining how best to measure success in achieving policy goals, and balancing the overall mission with customers' specific needs and demands. Indeed, customers can have multiple, even conflicting expectations. However, because of the diminished choice in government services and the power that government necessarily exercises over individuals' lives, customer service tactics confront substantially more difficult problems in the public sector. The bottom line for democratic government is accountability—control of public policy by elected officials—not market-like profits or citizen satisfaction. Customer service cannot substitute for the basic constitutional requirements of democratic government.

A 1999 survey of customer service in the U.S. federal government indicated that government agencies generally compared favorably with private organizations that had similar missions. The National Quality Research Center at the business school of the University of Michigan has been surveying private sector customers since 1994, but the 1999 survey represented the first application of its methodology to government. On a 100-point scale, the average customer satisfaction score for private sector service businesses was 71.9; government agencies scored a close 68.6. The center's report concluded that "government employees who have contact with the public receive high marks for courtesy and professionalism."[37]

Customer service has played an important role in government reform. In many countries citizens have received a powerful signal that their government is interested in improving its service to and relationship with them. Customer service also has transformed the behavior of government officials by shaking them out of their bureaucratic routine and making them focus on citizens' needs. Some managers have found customer service a useful tactic for breaking down bureaucratic walls and improving the integration of public services. However, at its core customer service is something of an enigma. As a reform tool it is both one of the most universal and one of the hardest to define and implement in government.

Unlike private companies, government agencies typically cannot choose their customers. In many government programs, especially those involving taxation and regulations, citizens cannot choose whether to deal with government; private sector comparisons therefore are suspect in these cases. The overall approach, however, has been useful in changing bureaucratic behavior.

Information Technology

The computer revolution has spread hand in hand with the global revolution in government management.

SPANNING BOUNDARIES. The promise of information technology lies in its ability to easily traverse organizational boundaries and allow quick, easy connections between citizens and government, regardless of which agencies are in charge of providing services. In many ways technology is the ultimate boundary-spanning technique. Consider the following examples gathered from around the globe:

—In the United States the Social Security Administration has made estimates of individuals' projected benefits available online at its website.

—Electronic filing of U.S. income tax returns became popular quickly, and taxpayers can now download forms and instructions from the IRS website.

—Denmark introduced a "paperless" income tax system, in which taxpayers do not have to file paper returns. The government reviews their earnings, calculates the taxes due, subtracts payments withheld from their salaries, and mails them a statement. Taxpayers who are due refunds receive a check along with the statement. If they owe more taxes, the amount due is rolled into the next year's withholding. If they want to make corrections to the statement, they can do so by telephone or online.

—Qatar created an award-winning national geographic information system based on information supplied from global positioning satellites. The information supports everything from land use planning to health assessments.

—In the Australian state of Victoria, citizens can use the "Vic Roads" kiosk project to register their cars and obtain driver's licenses. Kiosks are self-operated electronic systems stationed in public areas, such as shopping malls and building lobbies, which allow citizens to conduct business without having to visit government offices or deal directly with government officials. The system brings not only convenience but also choice to citizens, because it eliminates what surveys have shown to be the greatest complaint about the traditional licensing procedure: unflattering photos. Vic Roads allows drivers to pick the picture they like best. Government officials have concluded that in a country as vast as Australia, such electronic systems conquer "the tyranny of distance" and improve citizens' access to government. In addition, government officials do not have to be stationed in every small community throughout the country. The systems, which have spread throughout Australia's state and local governments, allow government to customize services to citizens as well as save money.

—Sweden's Kista project seeks both vertical and horizontal integration of a wide range of services and providers, regardless of whether they are national or local.

—Finland has centralized some judicial services once provided by municipalities, using information technology to improve the system.

—Britain's "life events" system, an effort to organize government services not by agency but by event or transaction, seeks to present seamless access to government, regardless of which level or branch of government provides the service.

CENTRALIZATION TO PROMOTE COORDINATION. Many information technology innovations are inherently centralizing. "Coordination," the OECD explains, "occurs at the point of service delivery."[38] To make things work seamlessly at the bottom, they must be carefully coupled from the top. Computer systems must be technically compatible and must rely on carefully integrated databases. The more local governments or individual national government agencies construct their own systems and build their own hardware, the greater the chance that the systems cannot easily be linked. Building effective links requires making—and sharing—basic decisions about systems, software, and database construction.

Other forces have enhanced and continue to enhance the trend toward centralization. As information technology became more central to the European Union, member states looked for basic standards to ensure compatibility of their data. Similarly, fear of the potential havoc that the

Y2K computer "bug" might wreak led many countries to share information and implement solutions so that their systems would continue to operate beyond December 31, 1999. Information technology is not cheap, and often the purchase orders for IT systems have come from high levels of government that, in return for their investment, have insisted on certain system standards.

TECHNICAL DIFFICULTIES AND CHALLENGES. Not surprisingly, big problems have accompanied the spread of computer-based systems. New York's new system to encode government food and benefits credits on electronic debit cards has suffered serious growing pains. Banks imposed large fees on users, eroding the value of the benefits. Many automatic teller machines (ATMs) refused to accept the cards, and the cards did not always work. Recipients complained that too many merchants did not accept them. Consequently, some recipients retreated to storefront check-cashing services, which charge even higher fees.

The problems in New York have not prevented other states from launching their own computer-based systems for disbursing public assistance. The California Department of Social Services, for example, planned its own ATM system to improve both the public assistance program's efficiency and the lives of recipients. "We're trying to remove the stigma of public assistance," explained Sidonie Squier, a spokeswoman for the agency. "[Beneficiaries] will swipe their cards at the [merchant's] check stand just like the rest of us. It should be an esteem builder."[39]

The new technology has been very popular in some applications. In Britain, citizens like photo driver's licenses because, as in the United States, they can be used as an all-purpose identification card. (And in California, for example, people who do not drive can request a nondriver's license—a government-issued photo ID.) Indeed, eleven of the fifteen European Union countries have issued identification cards. The European Union also is planning to issue medical smart cards, which would electronically encode information about an individual's blood type, medical history, and other medically useful information.[40]

Privacy concerns also have plagued these ambitious technology plans. For example, early in 1999 the British government proudly announced a new "smart card" for citizens. Within a decade citizens would be able to use this card to conduct all of their business with government. However, the government slowed implementation because citizens were worried that sensitive personal information might leak out of the system. In the United States, citizens in some states have led a campaign to prevent the disclosure of name, address, and telephone information in department of motor vehicles files. Generally these files are public records and thus can be viewed by anyone, but some states were selling the information to tele-marketers. State legislators are debating proposals to allow citizens to request that the information not be disclosed.

Computer systems present complex technical issues. It is one thing to create systems; it often is quite another to make them work reliably and predictably for users across organizational lines and, sometimes, with dif-ferent organizational cultures. Even more important, the spread of infor-mation technology raises daunting privacy issues: What information will government collect? Who will have access to the information? How can information be sped to those who ought to have access to it while keep-ing it out of the hands of those who ought not? These difficulties present short-term and some long-term problems for what surely will be a con-tinuing trend in government services. Information technology not only spans boundaries; "technology itself is a change agent."[41] It inevitably will change how government does what it does and how government employees understand their roles.

Regulatory Reform

Underlying all of these reform tactics in most nations has been a com-mitment to reduce government regulation. South Korea abolished almost half of its regulations. Costa Rica struck down barriers to entry in the pharmaceutical industry. The European Union has worked to coordinate regulations among its members—for example, by reducing the approvals required in each country for pharmaceuticals and encouraging single per-mitting for a wide range of commercial goods. Deregulation of the telecommunications and transportation industries has cut prices and spurred job creation in countries ranging from Japan and Finland to the United States and Germany. New Zealand abolished almost all agricul-tural support in the mid-1980s in the midst of the government's other reforms. Unemployment increased and some businesses failed, but within a decade the agricultural sector became internationally competitive and now contributes more to the economy than ever before. Deregulation of the Swedish taxi industry increased the supply of taxis and decreased waiting time. In Japan, telecommunications deregulation reduced prices by 41 percent.[42]

Deregulation is scarcely an immediate and automatic winner. Markets grow according to the rules in the environment in which they exist;

changing the rules shifts the balance among the players and creates different winners and losers. Moreover, the New Zealand case shows that restructuring markets can take some time and, in the meantime, impose substantial costs. Thus on one level, deregulation is about economic efficiency, but on another, it is quite clearly about politics and political redistribution. For those reasons an OECD assessment found that "the most important ingredient for successful regulatory reform is the strength and consistency of support at the highest political level. Ministers have a direct role to play in assuring that strong political leadership will overcome vested interests in both public and private sectors which benefit from the status quo and resist beneficial change."[43]

The political stakes involved in regulation and deregulation make piecemeal reform difficult and economically risky. Piecemeal reforms can stir up substantial political battles at each turn without fundamentally transforming markets; because of that, the most successful regulatory reforms have been comprehensive.

In many ways regulation is the prototypical symbol of traditional government. By contrast, deregulation has been a critical foundation of reform since the late 1970s. Its roots are partly economic—that is, it uses market forces to replace bureaucratic decisions. It is even more fundamentally political, because it uproots long-established interests worldwide that have shaped the rules of the game to their own benefit. The administrative strategy of deregulation cannot be separated from the political and economic issues it raises. Indeed, this is the most important lesson for other reform tactics as well: the setting of reforms—their broader political and economic context—cannot be ignored.

Policy, Management, and Governance

The global reform movement sought to reduce government's costs and increase its productivity, make government a friendlier partner to both citizens and businesses, and improve government managers' ability to manage. It was an ongoing effort to make government "work better and cost less," according to the NPR. Reformers around the world have celebrated its accomplishments, but they also have taken sober account of two basic problems. Prime Minister Jenny Shipley noted that after New Zealand's fifteen years of reform experience, "there is still much to do. . . . No government, no economy, can stand still. Reinventing government does not stop. It must be continual, forever demanding new benchmarks of performance to define value and improvement for people." And she observed that "reform fatigue and the power of vested interests will always be formidable obstacles."[44]

The fact that reform is never finished has been the most important lesson learned from the strategies and tactics of management reform. The reform movement has centered on administrative tools, which in the end have meaning only to the degree that they advance political goals; they have little power without political support. As the next chapter demonstrates, reform is deeply embedded in governance.

CHAPTER FIVE

Reform as Governance

The management reform movement has had a powerful effect on government action throughout the world as nations move into the twenty-first century. The level of activity—from New Zealand's vigorous efforts to reshape the state to those of many developing countries to accelerate their own transformations—has simply been remarkable. Perhaps never before have so many governments tried to change so much so fast in such similar ways.

Assessing whether those reforms have produced solid results is a different matter. Cynics have dismissed many of the reforms as nothing more than the latest fad. Indeed, the continual march of budgeting initiatives—from planning-based program budgets through zero-based budgets to quality- and results-driven budgets—has fueled the cynics' claims. Reforms often seem guaranteed only to breed more reforms.

Moreover, good data on what governments have attempted, let alone what they have accomplished, often have been scarce. One of the most remarkable aspects of the global reform movement is just how poor the documentation of the reforms themselves has been and how little effort has been invested in evaluating them—in part because the reforms have invariably had a strong political component. Elected officials launch reforms as part of a major initiative to reshape their government, but once they are launched, incentives are weak for following up to see whether the promised changes actually occur. When there has been analysis, fuzzy data have provoked political disputes over which reform claims are legitimate and which are overstated. For example, in 1999 a General

Accounting Office report questioned the $137 billion in cost savings claimed by NPR. Representative Dan Burton (R-Ind.) accused the Clinton administration of trying "to pad the numbers" and of "reinventing accounting rules." One administration official countered, "These are savings that took place," and concluded, "We frankly are proud of that."[1]

Moreover, reforms of government management are inevitably tied up with fundamental issues of policy and political and economic change. Not only is performing a separate assessment of management difficult, it also could prove trivial, since what citizens and elected officials care most about is the quality of life—not the quality of public management. Indeed, management matters only to the degree that it produces results. Assessing the global public management revolution therefore is fundamentally about assessing the broader trends of governance and policy. And given the very different patterns of governance and policy in developing nations, the issues often are subtly different there.

What impact have these reforms had? How have the big issues varied in less developed nations? This chapter addresses those questions.

Basic Puzzles

Few if any government leaders have launched management reforms simply to improve administration and service delivery. Those goals are important, but only in the context of strong political demands to save money. In most nations, it was the combination of the "works better" and "costs less" elements that drove the reforms.

However, gauging the cost savings of the reforms has been very difficult everywhere, for several reasons. First, it is impossible to know what decisions governments would have made otherwise, so there is no solid baseline for comparison. Second, despite many nations' investment in better cost accounting, most public accounting systems are inadequate for tracking the real cost of government programs and the link between inputs and results. Third, management reforms often are entangled in ongoing, high-profile political issues and ongoing, tumultuous political battles. Separating the management from the political issues usually is impossible, as the dispute between Representative Burton and Vice President Gore suggests. Indeed, the management reforms typically get the greatest attention when they yield politically important results. Such is the paradox of assessing management reforms: they become more visible and important as they become more commingled with political forces.

Comparative analysis of the leading administrative reform efforts suggests that they showed impressive gains in productivity. Analysis is incomplete at best, but anecdotal evidence, coupled with cross-national comparisons, indeed suggests that many nations succeeded in at least marginally improving government's ability to produce more and better government services at lower cost.[2] However, no good, reliable data are available in any country regarding the savings that the reforms produced.

What is the strongest indicator of success? Many nations have continued their reform efforts, despite pitched political battles and changes in government. Given the opportunity to drop the campaign, new governments in New Zealand, the United Kingdom, and the United States not only have persevered but also have launched new initiatives. Other nations that were not part of the first phase of the movement, like Denmark, have joined the fray. Whatever the difficulty of providing a strong analytical assessment of the results of reform, elected officials clearly see enough value in the effort to continue it even when confronted with easy exits.

Size of Government

In many nations one of the goals of the reform movement was to reduce the size of the public sector. But it is difficult to assess the success of public management reform in cutting government because government size, at least as measured by government spending as a share of the total economy, varies so greatly among the world's industrialized nations. As figure 5-1 shows, Sweden, Denmark, France, and Finland have relatively large public sectors, with government accounting for more than half of their gross domestic product (GDP). Ireland, Australia, and the United States, by contrast, have far smaller governments, accounting for just over one-third of GDP. (Note that those numbers include spending at all levels of government.) Making government smaller is thus a highly relative goal. The New Zealand government, which underwent perhaps the most radical transformation, remained much larger than other governments that also underwent reform (including the United States, Australia, and Ireland). Moreover, it remained larger than that of another major nation—Japan—which largely escaped the government reform movement.

The reform movement brought dramatic change to some countries in particular. Spending among the members of the Organization for Economic Cooperation and Development, the world's leading organization of industrialized nations, inched up slightly from 1987 to 2006, by just

Figure 5-1. *Government Spending as a Percent of GDP, 2006*

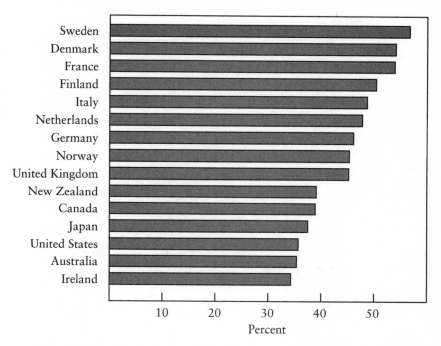

Percent

Source: Compiled from data from Organization for Economic Cooperation and Development, *Economic Outlook Database* (2004). Amounts are estimated for 2006.

over 0.1 percent. Some nations used the reform process to make major reductions in government spending, including Ireland (34 percent), New Zealand (27 percent), the Netherlands (18 percent), and Canada (16 percent). Spending in some nations—notably those that had not undergone major reforms—increased: Finland (4 percent), France (4 percent), and Japan (19 percent). Government spending in the United Kingdom increased, by almost 4 percent, despite the reforms, although there were substantial reductions in the government workforce. In the United States, government spending at all levels shrank by 3.4 percent (see figure 5-2).

In some nations, reforms brought even more fundamental changes in government employment (see figure 5-3). In the United Kingdom government employment (measured as a share of all employees) shrank dramatically, by 42 percent. Ireland cut its employment by 28 percent. In the

Figure 5-2. *Government Outlays as a Share of GDP:*
Percent Change from 1987–2006

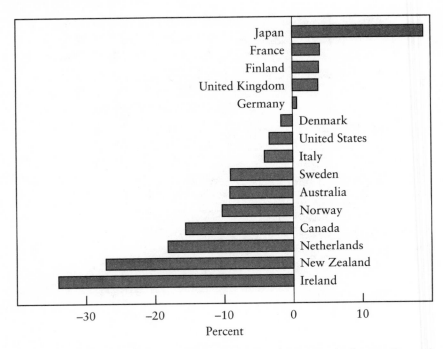

Source: Compiled from data from Organization for Economic Cooperation and Development, *Economic Outlook Database* (2004). Amounts are estimated for 2006.

United States, overall government employment fell by 2 percent. In France, which did not undertake major reforms, government employment rose 4 percent.

In general, aggressive government reforms did indeed bring about a smaller government. The correlation, however, is sometimes weak. In the United Kingdom, where government employment fell significantly, government spending did not. In Sweden, which launched some of the world's most comprehensive budget reforms, spending shrank only slightly in the 1990s, by 1 percent. However, the government's reforms were not aimed at shrinking government but at reducing costs to maintain the nation's welfare state. Sweden leads the industrialized world in government spending.

Figure 5-3. *Percent Change in Public Employment since 1985*[a]

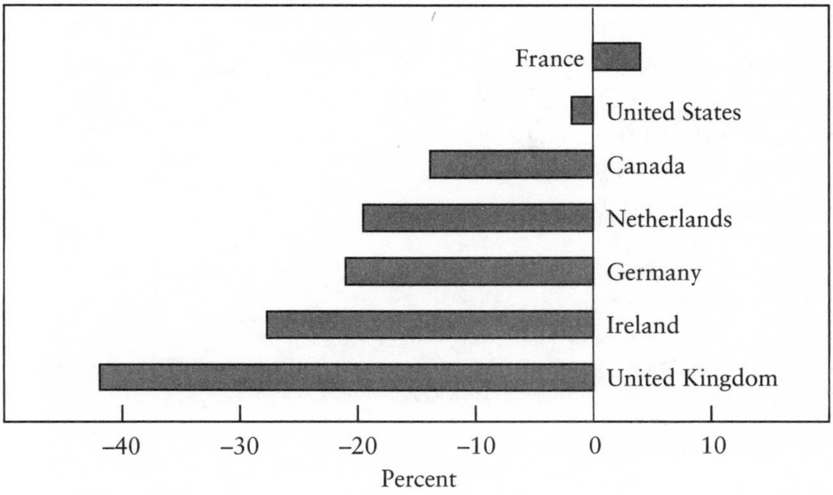

Source: Compiled from data from Organization for Economic Cooperation and Development, OECD Public Management Service (2001).

a. Public employment as a share of total employment. Change from 1985 to 1998 for Ireland; to 1997 for France; and to 1999 for all others.

Nevertheless, it is important to emphasize the fact that management reform is not associated with any particular size of government. The impetus toward reform did not come from the largest governments, and governments after reform did not tend toward any particular size. What *is* remarkable is that the government downsizing movement hit so many countries simultaneously, regardless of the comparative size of their government. The reform movement grew out of a larger need to respond to the rising taxpayer rebellion at the size of government and to retool government to work more effectively in an era of economic globalization.

Trust in Government

In most nations the reformers explicitly pledged to improve citizens' trust in government. Although the decline of civic trust in American government is well-documented, cross-national comparisons are difficult because researchers rarely have asked the same questions in the same way at the same time.[3] However, through research such as the World Values

Table 5-1. *Changes in Citizen Opinions of Government Performance in the 1990s*

Performance area	N	Number of countries		Overall mean percent change
		Increasing	Decreasing	
General system performance	12	4	8	–7
Confidence in parliament	22	3	15	–12
Confidence in government	9	3	5	–12
Satisfaction with the democratic process				
European Union[a]	15	7	4	–0.3
Central and eastern European nations	18	7	7	0.0

Source: From analysis by Pippa Norris, "Mapping Political Support in the 1990s: A Global Analysis," in *Critical Citizens: Global Support for Democratic Governance*, edited by Pippa Norris (Oxford University Press, 1999), table 2.15.

a. The mean is heavily skewed by Portugal's 35.5 percent decrease. If Portugal is removed from the sample, the mean is a 2.4 percent increase.

Survey, researchers in many nations have found similar, troubling trends. In almost all industrialized nations, citizens' responses indicate declining confidence in public institutions. The drop has been especially sharp in Germany, Japan, Italy, the United States, and even Sweden.[4]

Robert Putnam, Susan Pharr, and Russell Dalton reported that confidence in political institutions declined during the 1990s in eleven of the fourteen nations that they examined. Declines were especially sharp in Canada, Germany, Sweden, the United Kingdom, and the United States. Only Denmark, Iceland, and the Netherlands varied from the overall trend. In 1985, for example, 48 percent of Britons expressed quite a lot of confidence in the House of Commons, but by 1995 the percentage had decreased by half. Similar or greater declines plagued most other major democracies.[5] Pippa Norris found that public confidence in most public institutions declined during the 1990s (table 5-1). Citizens remain committed to democracy as a form of government, but they are unhappy about the way it is operating in their own countries. This discontent, claims Norris, has proven a powerful impetus for reforming government.[6]

On the surface, these and similar survey results are scarcely a ringing endorsement of government reform. There is no evidence that extensive management and political reform efforts have halted the downward slide of public confidence in government. However, it is likely that public confidence is a lagging indicator of the effects of reform: it might take long and sustained improvement to register with citizens and to increase public confidence in government. It is also possible that although reform might not increase public confidence, it might help stem the long-term pattern of decline. Indeed, the decline of trust in government began decades before the global movement toward management reform, and in many countries the movement began as part of a broader strategy to reverse the decline. At the least, the global reform movement is a symptom of—and a reaction to—the decline of public confidence in government institutions and performance. But despite the hopes of many reformers, there is little hard evidence that public management reform has in fact restored the public's trust in government and its institutions.

Assessment

Despite efforts that span years, even decades, clear indicators of the success of the public management reform movement are hard to find. The administrative efforts inevitably are tied up with political decisions. Citizens seem to trust their institutions less than they used to; whether the reform movement has helped to restore their trust is unclear. Moreover, it is difficult, if not impossible, to separate confidence in elected decisionmakers from confidence in the unelected administrators who carry out their decisions.

Two strong characteristics of the administrative reform movement demonstrate its power. First, the movement has spread throughout much of the world. Government officials champion reform because they believe that it is likely to help. Second, no government that has launched a reform movement has ever given up on it. Although changes of government have brought shifts in strategy and tactics, throughout the 1990s there were no retreats. Officials continue to reform their governments because they seem to believe that it gives them political leverage—and perhaps because the managerial challenges of modern government leave them no choice.

Challenges for Developing Nations

Developing nations have embraced reform to help cope with governance problems and to speed the development process. Their problems have been substantial. Public officials in Ghana, for example, talk passionately about their need to shrink the size of government to improve its efficiency, reduce taxes, and stimulate the growth of the private sector. Accomplishing that goal means reducing the government payroll and privatizing government services. However, the government has long been a major source of employment in the country, and reducing the payroll before creating new private sector jobs would increase unemployment. The government has debated privatization, but it is difficult to spin off public enterprises before the private sector has the financial and managerial capacity to absorb them. Moreover, the new form of government that would result would require of its employees managerial skills that are in short supply. But government officials feel they have little choice but to move quickly along the road to reform; to do otherwise is to risk slipping behind in the global race for capital and economic growth. Thus they face the task of reinventing their government while simultaneously inventing and strengthening basic social institutions.

It is little wonder that the reformers' experience, especially in New Zealand, has had such appeal. The World Bank and other international organizations have touted the New Zealand reforms. The New Zealand reformers themselves have been missionaries, traveling around the world to talk about what they accomplished, and because New Zealand's economy has moved from stagnation to strong growth, their ideas are especially attractive. Although the rhetoric of the reforms has spread around the world, Allen Schick has found that only a handful of industrialized nations and just a few developing countries (for example, Mongolia) have pursued the essential features of the system. Why? Schick argues: "On the whole, industrial and developing countries have not implemented such reforms because the reforms are beyond their reach or do not fit their current needs."[7]

Preconditions for Reform

Schick quite persuasively argues that New Zealand has contributed a great deal to both the theory and practice of public management. However, making the reforms work depends on "important preconditions" that many developing nations—and even some industrialized nations—do not possess.[8] The New Zealand reforms, as well as many other prescriptions for change, depend on having in place both public and private institutions that have the capacity to accommodate reform. In short, management reform is a matter of integrating administrative efforts with the fabric of each nation's government and civil society. Enrique Iglesias, president of the Inter-American Development Bank, observed, "We do not question whether we need more or less state intervention. It is not a matter of simply downsizing but of rightsizing. The key, as we all know, is the quality of government."[9]

Former World Bank president James D. Wolfensohn contends that development and reform depend on four structures:

—*Good governance.* "You have got to have governments that have the capacity, have trained people, have clear and transparent laws, and where there is a confrontation at the very highest level of issues of corruption. If you don't have that, you have very little chance of succeeding in your development exercise."

—*A justice system that works.* "You need laws that protect property rights, you need a contract system, you need bankruptcy laws, you need protection of human rights, varying with the country, and you need a justice system that will be clean and honest."

—*A financial system that works.* "Particularly after [the financial crises in] Indonesia and Thailand and South Korea and Mexico and many others, . . . you had better be sure you have a financial system that works—not just financial institutions, but a financial system that is supervised, monitored, controlled, and with people on both sides who are trained."

—*A social system that works.* "You need a social system . . . that can protect the weak, the old, the children, the disabled and can do something for the people who are out of work. That social system need not be an American-style social system, or British or German—it can be a tribal system, a familial system—but you need to have something that can take care of people who are suffering or aged."

A country without these four structures, Wolfensohn concluded, is "like a rowboat with a big hole in it." He added:

It is impossible, for example, to privatize in a nation without a well-developed system of competitive markets. New Zealand–style management-by-contract systems—or, indeed, any system of public sector contracting out—cannot work in a society without a well-developed system of contract law. Output-based management controls fail if the government does not have a strong budgeting system to set goals and an accounting system to track results. The government reform movement puts especially heavy pressure on government managers, who not only must do more with less. They must also build new capacity to find imaginative ways to do things they have never done before.[10]

In short, public management reform is not only a job for the public sector; the central reform strategies require broad participation from members of society in setting goals and, in many cases, close partnership between the governmental and nongovernmental sectors. "The emergence of open, robust markets is as much a precondition for modernizing the public sector as it is for developing the private economy," Schick argues. Moreover, he observes, efforts to reform government that are out of sync with norms elsewhere in society are doomed to fail: "It is highly unlikely that government will operate by the book when rules and regulations are routinely breached in private transactions." Especially in many developing countries, Schick contends, citizens and public officials alike must cope with red tape, rule-bound bureaucracies, bad policies, and poor government performance. But often the culture of both government and the private sector is informal, and informality can help everyone cope with such systems. However, informality also can breed corruption and more inefficiency and can frustrate efforts to impose management reforms of the sort popularized elsewhere.[11]

New Zealand's contract-driven system is the most formalized governance system in the world. The stunning transformation of the New Zealand economy, even though performance lagged in the late 1990s, lured many governments to consider mimicking its tactics. So too did the dramatic downsizing of its government. Without first building a private sector with the capacity to follow the public sector reforms and then developing a more formal and transparent system of governance, Schick warns, developing countries risk "taking shortcuts that turn into dead ends."[12] His warning is not a prescription for either maintaining the status quo or adopting a go-slow process. Singapore and Chile moved rapidly to improve both economic development and public management. Singapore moved from a traditional line-item budget to a system that incorporated important elements of the New Zealand system. The lesson for developing nations is that the public sector cannot be reformed without reforming the private sector in tandem.

For the leaders of many developing nations, that is a bitter conclusion. They keenly feel the harsh heat of global economic competition and the desire of their people for rapid improvement in their living conditions.

The argument that they must first rebuild their civic and government institutions before moving more aggressively to improve the lives of their citizens can seem like a permanent, paternalistic condemnation to second-class status. On one level, of course, Schick is right: there can be no contract-based system of management without a system of public law that structures and enforces contracts. But development experts are working hard to devise systems of institutional reform that allow nations to speed up the learning curve for both public and private institutions and to find intermediate reform strategies that permit rapid progress. Of all the issues surrounding public management reform, however, the puzzle about how to press ahead with aggressive reforms while building basic institutions might well prove the most difficult—and the most important.

Policy and Management

Despite large-scale government downsizing, reformers nevertheless believed firmly in a strong, important role for government. Unlike some doctrinaire conservatives who sought simply to shrink government as much as possible, the reformers were pragmatists who believed that government has an important role to play in society but that it needs to play its role in a different way. Canada's Clerk of the Privy Council and Secretary to the Cabinet Jocelyne Bourgon argued, "Less government is not a guarantee of better government."[13] Indeed, Iglesias stated, "We do not necessarily believe that government should govern less nor should it try to govern with fewer resources. The pivotal role of the private sector, the engine of growth, is not the answer to all of society's problems."[14]

The quest for reform often has meant redefining government's role. In Bolivia the government has expanded citizens' access to basic services, such as electricity and telephone service. It has developed "four pillars": opportunity, equity, strengthening of governmental institutions, and dignity. Minister of Housing and Basic Services Amparo Ballivain explained, "The steps taken in my country include the rolling back of the state from controlling what we call the 'commanding heights of the economy' to acting as a facilitator." The government has privatized publicly owned enterprises and has worked to shift government's role toward promoting market-driven growth.[15] The Polish government has pursued similar reforms, built on the principle of subsidiarity: devolution and decentralization of government power to bring it closer to the people and enhance the ability of the private sector to perform well.

Reform: Convergence or Divergence?

The management reform movement has spread around the world with remarkable speed. Reformers in every nation have pursued the movement in different ways, with bold rhetoric about reinvention and reform tailored to the special managerial and political problems that they face. However, as I suggested in chapters 2 and 3, the reforms have tended to originate in one of two fundamentally different philosophies: Westminster or American.[16]

The Westminster-style strategy began by redefining what government ought to do and led to the privatization of functions that officials concluded government could not or should not do. It brought about new budgeting and personnel policies along with the reengineering of organizational processes and internal contracting strategies. The Westminster governments have launched sweeping, comprehensive reforms that sought to restructure government and what it does, from top to bottom.

The American-style strategy sought cheaper, more effective government without shrinking the scope of government activities. It has attempted to incorporate the best practices of businesses into government's operations, from customer service to a focus on results. Its reforms have been incremental rather than sweeping and comprehensive.

The Nordic countries have combined these two approaches in their quest for the same goal. They have used sweeping budgetary reforms characteristic of Westminster-style reform to sustain the basic welfare state. However, their efforts were consistent with the broad American strategy of avoiding fundamental transformations in the scale and scope of government.

Graham Scott, the architect of the New Zealand reforms, has argued that these two strategies may be converging. He suggests, "For most of the world, the late twentieth century has been about reducing the scope of government. But this process must inevitably slow down." Sooner or later, government will shrink to a point beyond which it cannot—for political, economic, and pragmatic reasons—shrink any further. All governments eventually will reach a size at which they are likely to stay. At that point, nations will face the common problem of making their government programs work better and cost less. Scott concludes, "Over time, the rest of us will look more and more like the United States, as the problems of what the government is going to do become less urgent and we deal with them by marginal adjustments rather than sudden and radical change, and focus more on the steady processes of improvement around the organizations that will persist."[17]

The Case for Convergence

Scott's argument focuses on several important issues. With the spread of public management innovations, is the reform movement increasingly centered on certain core questions? Is there convergence on public management reforms? Are reforms moving more toward the American version?

There is in fact strong evidence for convergence. First, the initial phase of reform in many nations focused on shrinking the size and role of the state. The American downsizing effort, except in the federal civil service, was virtually nonexistent, while other nations followed the Westminster approach, privatizing substantial government-owned enterprises. In most nations, however, whatever downsizing that is likely to happen has happened. Their efforts have produced governments of vastly different sizes, but all nations face the task of effectively managing the government that remains. Moreover, more elected officials have made a strong case for assigning a positive role to the government that is left. Many nations are converging on a recognition of the twin puzzles of redefining government's role and size and of building the capacity to make it work effectively.

Second, the reform movement has shifted the focus of many governments away from inputs (money spent or people employed by government) to results (outputs or outcomes). With the Government Performance and Results Act and the Bush administration's management reform agenda, the United States launched perhaps the world's most ambitious results-oriented system. How well government managers will master the program's technical details and how elected officials will deal with the result measures are anything but clear, but the system at least creates a novel process. The New Zealand government has led the way in output measurement, while other Westminster nations have developed related systems, from customer-driven measures to private sector–derived benchmarks. Elected officials are unlikely to abandon inputs. In most nations, their job is to define public goals and determine how best to use society's resources. Budgets and public hiring are the coin of the political realm. However, governments today are paying far more attention to the results of their spending programs.

Third, many nations have devolved substantial responsibility for domestic policy to their local governments. In federal systems such as those of Australia, Canada, Germany, and especially the United States, devolution has long been a central part of governance. However, other nations have spun off responsibility to lower levels. In the United Kingdom, referendums in Scotland and Wales led to substantial devolution. The Swedish government has given new responsibility to local governments, and the South Korean government has debated more devolution as well. The shift of responsibility for managing programs—and, as in the case of American welfare reform, for shaping policy—has marked many government reform strategies.

Fourth, institutions in civil society, especially private companies and nonprofit organizations, are playing a stronger role in service delivery. In many nations reform meant downsizing, and downsizing brought significant privatization. In the United States the government had relatively few enterprises to privatize, but the government significantly expanded its reliance on private and nonprofit contractors. As other nations sought to increase their own operating flexibility, especially in Canada and Germany, they too looked to contractors. The use of nongovernmental agents to deliver public services increased significantly in other nations, and the movement showed strong evidence of spreading.

Fifth, government managers are looking for ideas that they can adopt—"best practices"—from other nations and the private sector. The American reinvention movement derived many of its most important elements, especially the strong focus on customer service and information technology, from the experiences of private companies. In fact, Vice President Gore titled his 1997 report on the NPR's progress *Businesslike Government: Lessons Learned from America's Best Companies*.[18] Osborne and Gaebler's *Reinventing Government* celebrated an "entrepreneurial spirit" borrowed heavily from private companies. The authors were quite emphatic that "government cannot be run like a business." However, they identified ten basic principles that "underlie success for any institution in today's world—public, private, or nonprofit."[19] Trading reform ideas often has been troublesome. Reformers have been tempted to pick the ideas that they like and ignore the hard ones, and they frequently have failed to build the infrastructure required for the most difficult ventures. Governments often borrow from the private sector without stopping to consider the profound differences between them; moreover, governments have borrowed private sector ideas just as the private sector has found them unworkable or inadequate.[20] With the high-speed communication permitted by the Internet and the heavy pressure for continued cost cutting and improved productivity, the constant search for management ideas will likely continue around the globe.

Points of Divergence

Despite significant points of convergence, important structural differences probably will prevent the American experience from reshaping global management reform. The New Zealand and similar Westminster reforms sought to clarify policy goals and administrative responsibility for achieving those goals and to design measures to gauge how well managers achieved them. Those reforms gave managers great operating flexibility in exchange for tough accountability for their performance. In practice there often was considerable slippage between the rhetoric and reality. Moreover, few nations were as aggressive as New Zealand in pursuing that approach. Nevertheless the driving logic of the Westminster reforms sought to define responsibility sharply, drawing clear lines between goals and results, between inputs and outputs, and between policymakers and managers.

The American governmental system, by contrast, is built on a constitutional system of separated powers and shared responsibility. Especially in domestic policy, responsibility for program management is shared by the federal, state, and local governments—and between government and its nongovernmental partners. Within government, responsibility for decisions is shared among the executive, legislative, and judicial branches. The rough-and-tumble politics of the American system reinforces the constitutional features. These elements would make it difficult for American governments to match the requirements of the Westminster reforms. For the Westminster governments, moving toward the fuzzy responsibilities of the American system would undermine the very reforms that they have developed.

In short, the Westminster-style reforms build on drawing sharp boundaries. The American system traditionally has avoided such clear lines. Moreover, the American strategies and tactics of the last half of the twentieth century have blurred existing lines even further. Governments at all levels have relied more on contracting out for everything from defense to social service projects. The growth of Medicaid and Medicare in the 1970s and 1980s accelerated that trend, and welfare reform in the 1990s brought new nongovernmental partners into the service delivery system. Indeed, American reforms are perhaps most distinctive for their deep integration of governance into the very fabric of civil society.

The Westminster governments have moved toward the use of civil society in the governance system. Non-Westminster parliamentary systems from South Korea to eastern Europe have considered such a move themselves. In federal systems such systems of shared power have come more easily and have moved more quickly, especially in Australia and Canada. But this issue frames a central puzzle for any notion that the reforms are converging. American reforms are moving toward greater blurring of the responsibilities for policies within government—and of government's and civil society's responsibility for managing them. Despite the growing importance of civil society in other nations, many of the reforms have moved in the opposite direction, toward more attempts to clarify the boundaries between policy and administration and between government and society. In fact, the "new public management" (the academic theory that supported Westminster-style reforms) was largely an effort to reinstate the distinction between policymaking and policy execution that American scholars spent most of the twentieth century trying to erase.

The question of convergence and divergence remains open. Will non-American systems, especially among the Westminster nations, slide away from their efforts to draw sharp boundaries and more toward American-style sharing of power? Will American reformers move more toward the agency-style approach of the Westminster governments and give government's agents more responsibility in exchange for greater accountability? The questions that remain guarantee continued debate and ongoing reform. If nothing else, the experience of the global reform movement establishes ongoing reform as the foundation for government in the twenty-first century.

Nevertheless, there are intriguing signs that governments around the world are moving to new systems of accountability built on the measurement of outcomes; to new approaches to service delivery based on partnerships with for-profit and nonprofit organizations; to aggressive innovations in information technology; and to new strategies of engaging citizens in governance. The debate over convergence of reforms will continue. What is even more notable is the continuing energetic, evolutionary character of public management reforms in so many nations of the world. In many cases, the reforms bear scant resemblance to the first stages of reform in the early 1980s—except in their continuing search for a government that works better and costs less.

CHAPTER SIX

Governance for the Twenty-First Century

The reform of public management has become a center-piece of governance in the twenty-first century. It has become so stylish that governments feel obliged to launch reforms, no matter how modest their own investment in the effort. Having launched reforms, they feel further obliged to trumpet their success, for no government can afford to admit that any important initiative is a failure—especially one devoted to transforming its own operations. And when a new government takes office, it finds itself under inescapable pressure to shrink costs, improve service, and deliver more programs to taxpayers.

Predictably, such motivations have generated a great deal of cynicism and suspicion. Have the reforms really accomplished anything? Why do they endure? And what connections do such management efforts have with political life?[1]

Most discussions of public management reform begin with a flawed premise: that management reform is fundamentally about management. Indeed, discussions about management reform often quickly turn into arcane debates about the relative value of output and outcome measures, strategies for culture change, and the importance of reengineering organizational processes compared with "soft" people-based approaches.

But management reform is not fundamentally about management. Elected officials do not pursue management reform for its own sake but because they believe that it helps them achieve a broader political purpose. Greater efficiency has real value to officials because it can help them reduce taxes or increase services. Greater effectiveness matters because citizens are less likely to complain about programs that they think work well. Even for managers, management reform is not only about management. Management reform requires strong political direction and support; reform led only by internal reformers is inherently and sharply limited. Managers have little incentive to pay careful attention to performance measures if elected officials do not indicate that they, too, are paying attention. But measuring results is always a risky proposition; it can shed unwelcome light on mistakes and draw political attack from those seeking to eliminate or radically change programs that they dislike.

The same is true of reform in developing nations, perhaps even more so. Developing nations face the challenge of accelerating internal economic progress while creating strategies to compete effectively in the global economy. In addition to devising new management strategies, they must transform their political institutions. For political and administrative transformations to succeed, developing nations frequently must build new social structures, legal systems, and market arrangements. Like industrialized nations, they must understand not only what the state can do but what it cannot do. As Inter-American Development Bank president Enrique Iglesias said:

> Allow me to let you in on a little secret that we have learned in our work in reform of the state. Reform of the state is essentially a political issue. It has succeeded in countries in Latin America where there is a general consensus for the need for change. To accomplish this consensus, and where the Bank can play a catalytic role, it is essential that there be a clear vision and acceptance of the role of the state and its limits. Political leadership and political parties are necessary in order to help articulate the goals of the country and therefore the proper role of the state in pursuit of those goals.[2]

Public management thus is inevitably about politics. Management reform is also about political reform, and political reform cuts directly to the core issues of the relationship between government and society. Viewed that way, however, the subject may be so broad as to make precise prescriptions impossible. However, to focus on management only as management ignores the central issues of the reform movement—and the factors that determine how well it actually works.

Reforming public management is not simply a matter of transforming administration with new structures, processes, and (often fewer) people.

The New Zealand reforms required elected officials to define what they wanted to accomplish, create incentives for performance, and measure how well managers accomplished their goals. Thus the accountability of top managers to elected officials was based on negotiated contracts, not on the traditional system of authority.

In the United States, the Government Performance and Results Act (GPRA) required government managers to define explicitly the goals of their programs. It forced an uncommon discussion about what federal programs ought to achieve. American welfare reform devolved most decisions to the states and substantial operating responsibility to private companies and nonprofit organizations. Although for decades the American government had relied heavily on nonprofit organizations to deliver social services, the scope and responsibility of contracting out under welfare reform lay far beyond what government, in the United States or elsewhere, had ever before attempted in social service programs.

Public management reform is about strengthening the ability of elected officials to produce results. It requires strong links between government administrators and elected officials. Moreover, it is not only about reforming the public sector. In some countries, including the United Kingdom and New Zealand, the reforms have involved substantial privatization of government enterprises. The private sector had to absorb those enterprises. Government had to expand its traditional services and find new ways of making markets more competitive. In nations from China to Germany, nonprofit organizations are playing a stronger role in the system. Public management reform is as much about politics as management. It is as much about the private and nonprofit sectors as it is about government. To a growing degree, the work of government is done only partly by government. Government performance depends strongly on the relationship of government administration with the rest of government and of government with nongovernmental partners.

Patterns in Reform

It is tempting but inaccurate to think of the global public management revolution as a single movement. It has been different in every nation that has attempted reform, but three broad strategies nevertheless have emerged.

Some nations, including France and Germany, have launched relatively *modest reforms*. Others, like the United States, have pursued steady,

Table 6-1. *Patterns of Public Management Reform*

Pattern	Examples	Positive features	Negative features
Modest	France Germany	Government is seen to be taking action.	Reform may produce activity but no real results. Important problems may go without fundamental solutions. Citizens may become cynical about the effort.
"Big bang"	New Zealand Slovak Republic	Crisis creates the political will necessary for reform, which provides a response to the crisis. Top-down strategic approach tends to be easier to pursue than bottom-up reform.	Instinct for quick reaction risks recycling past efforts—and replicating past problems. Solutions imported from other contexts (private sector, other nations) may prove a poor fit. Rapid, radical change may produce unintended consequences.
Incremental	United States	Slower pace of reform affords opportunities to learn. Slower reform improves ability to design reforms to manage complexity.	Creating the critical mass necessary for action is more difficult. It is harder to build and sustain political support. It is easy to slide into complacency.

incremental change, which sometimes has been sweeping in scope but more limited in political energy. Yet others, including New Zealand in the 1980s and the Slovak Republic in the 1990s, have pursued aggressive reforms that amount to fundamental transformation—something akin to a *"big bang"* in governance. Those efforts have had dramatically different strategies, and they also have produced widely different patterns, as table 6-1 shows.

Modest reforms create the appearance of action without actually delivering substantially different results. While they do not significantly disturb the system, they do risk feeding citizens' cynicism by promising things that the system does not deliver.

"Big-bang" reforms tend to be adopted as a quick response to a major crisis. Crises may generate greater political will to act and greater acceptance on the part of citizens of big change. But the effort to deploy big changes quickly can mean that officials reach for ideas that already are in play, which can risk relying on past approaches and failing to devise new solutions to new and future problems.

Incremental reforms can move a nation forward, providing opportunities to learn and fine-tune the changes along the way. But the slow pace of change can make it difficult to build and sustain political support. That creates a profound paradox: incremental reforms can offer significant potential for long-term improvement, but they also can be the hardest to maintain, since both citizens and elected officials are likely to question how small changes can solve the obvious big problems.

Moreover, the reform process has revealed several deeper issues: the importance of crises in galvanizing action, the risks of reform fatigue, the gap between developed and less-developed nations, the use of performance information, and the larger puzzles of accountability.

A Focus on Crisis

Reforms—especially the largest and most aggressive management reforms—have tended to appear most often when things go wrong or when the political stakes are high. Sometimes that has occurred when a nation faces economic collapse (as was the case in New Zealand) or a new government wants to effect a radical shakeup of existing policies (as was the case with the Thatcher government in the United Kingdom). The American reforms were a response to the political threat that the Clinton administration felt from Ross Perot as well as a result of the administration's search for the center in American politics. The hotter the heat, the more likely a government is to cobble together existing ideas to shape the reform. However, the bigger the problem, the less capable the existing inventory of ideas is likely to be in solving it. Big changes often require innovative thinking, and that is difficult to do in the midst of a megacrisis. Indeed, the deeper the crisis, the harder it is to move beyond symbolic to real change.

Reform Fatigue

Over the last fifteen years, many nations have seen a parade of management reforms go by. New governments have arrived, announced new initiatives, and issued new calls to action. Often managers within the government tire under the burden of constant change. As they have found, it is difficult to run the government management marathon at the sprinter's pace of a new government's need to act.

Modernization Gap

The leaders of less-developed nations keenly feel the ambitions of their citizens for economic growth. That lures them to adopt the core principles of public management reform—greater devolution of responsibility to frontline managers in exchange for closer assessment of their performance, along with more coordination of public services and greater reliance on instruments like contracts. As Schick has argued, however, reform often requires more capacity than their systems of public management and civil law can support. The efforts of some nations offer a partial answer. The Slovak Republic, for example, devised a two-stage approach: the first, aggressive stage involved getting the nation's vertical structures working properly (by improving leadership and capacity in the government bureaucracy, increasing efforts to root out corruption, and strengthening systems of public law), and the second stage involved connecting the vertical structures with stronger horizontal structures (including stronger service coordination and network management). The difficulty lies in encouraging such two-step reform without, in appearance or in fact, subjecting developing nations to a widening income gap.

Use of Performance Information

If there is convergence anywhere on the management reform front, it is in the central role that many nations have created for performance data, especially about program outcomes. The logic is simple and powerful: measure better what government does, and it will be easier to hold public administrators accountable for their performance and elected officials accountable for their leadership. As Christopher Pollitt has found, however, there is little evidence for that conclusion.[3] In fact, politicians and citizens seldom actually use performance information. And in arguing about the potential of performance data, reformers rarely stop to examine what actually happens with the data. As a result, little is known about how the ambitious assumptions about the power of performance information compare with its actual use.

Performance information does not always arrive in a form that top decisionmakers can digest or in ways that serve their immediate needs. A

2005 report by the U.S. Government Accountability Office (GAO) found that the emerging federal performance management system "enhanced agencies' flexibility and incentives to make trade-offs necessary to increase efficiency and responsiveness." NASA officials, in particular, welcomed the increased information and budget flexibility that the Bush management agenda brought. However, the GAO concluded, "budget changes did not meet the needs of some executive branch managers and congressional appropriations committees." Congressional staff members preferred the existing budget structures. They tended to focus on program spending and how it was distributed; the performance documents focused on strategic and performance goals. Congress had not been a partner in creating the new system, and its members and key staff did not find that the executive-driven system satisfied their needs. GAO concluded that "infusing a performance perspective into budget decisions may only be achieved when the underlying performance information becomes more credible, accepted, and used by all major decision makers."[4]

No matter what managerial advantages might flow from management reforms, elected officials often have been disappointed with their political results. Despite widespread support for the goal of making government smaller and making it work better, efficiency improvements are difficult to achieve, often entail substantial front-end costs in exchange for long-run benefits, and take time to implement. Gathering evidence on the cost savings of management reforms appears to be easy, but in practice turns out to be difficult indeed. Moreover, finding big savings often requires reducing public services or changing the ways in which citizens receive them. These issues create a difficult political setting for management reform. Improvements can be real, but the fiscal payoffs can seem puny in comparison with the rhetoric. Big fiscal payoffs frequently require trade-offs that citizens are reluctant to make.

Whey, then, do elected officials continue to insist on doing things that so often seem to have weak political payoffs? It surely is not because they are ignorant of history. Rather, it tends to be because management reforms serve other important political ends.

First, elected officials often are eager to put their imprint on the government, especially to signal to the bureaucracy that a new person is in charge. The announcement of new reform initiatives conveys a strong signal. When Bush took over from Clinton, for example, he immediately shut down Gore's "reinventing government" office and announced his own management reforms, thereby signaling stronger top-level attention to management and a stronger link to the budgetary process. But the reform process focuses sharp attention on a fundamental problem: the need for a stable, expert bureaucracy that responds to the needs of all elected officials—especially the executive—regardless of the politics of the particular administration in power.

Second, such signals do more than create symbols. They provide a counterbalance to other powerful pulls on government agencies. In the United States, for example, new presidents not only need to separate themselves from their predecessors, they also need to fight the continuing battle between the White House and Capitol Hill over who shapes bureaucratic behavior. Executive departments often find themselves caught in a tug of war between the president and Congress, and presidents have used managerial reforms to try to tip the balance in their favor.

Third, in an era when more and more of the government budget is "uncontrollable," driven by social welfare programs and long-term commitments over which elected officials have little immediate influence, any tool that offers even modest leverage is welcome. The bureaucracies that elected officials are charged with overseeing are increasingly complex and subject to many centrifugal forces. Even if their public statements rarely reflect the fact, elected executives are realistic about the potential of large-scale reforms. They typically are grateful for any marginal influence over what has become a vast, sprawling process.

Finally, the typical view of management reforms—that they involve big announcements followed by erosion of interest and negligible effects, followed in turn by repetition of the same cycle in the next government—is inaccurate. In fact, many reforms have had lasting impacts, although they may not make the headlines. The much-maligned "planning-programming-budgeting system" introduced by Robert McNamara and his Kennedy administration whiz kids continues to influence Pentagon budgets. Gore's customer-service initiatives have transformed everything from the way the IRS communicates with taxpayers to the Social Security Administration's efforts to strengthen its telephone service. The same is true in other nations that have launched management reforms. Although new governments often begin by publicly sweeping away the reforms of their predecessor, in reality many reforms endure and some have had long-term impacts.

In sum, the reform process works more like a ratchet than a pendulum, with government's capacity increased one step at a time. Sometimes the ratchet slips back. Sometimes reformers struggle over who controls how big the steps are and in what direction they ought to move. But it is difficult to dispute the proposition that public management reforms have made many governments more efficient and effective. But the politics underlying this movement have proven complex.

Accountability

From the New Zealand system of management contracts to the Bush management agenda, much of the reform process has built on an effort to strengthen accountability by clarifying responsibility. On the other hand, the process often has been undermined by the increasingly networked nature of government programs, with shared responsibility for increasingly ambitious goals and complex systems. From the United Kingdom's "no wrong door" initiative to e-government strategies, reformers increasingly are devising strategies for producing results in programs in which multiple organizations, inside and outside government, have a piece of the action.

This tendency toward blurring of boundaries and sharing of responsibility flies in the face of the mass media's interest in telling big, complex stories in simple, digestible form. When problems occur, the tendency—especially in television news, throughout the world—is for reporters to ask why the government did not prevent them and to seek a responsible official to explain. Accountability has increasingly become defined by the lens of the camera. Government officials, not surprisingly, have invested more energy in trying to communicate through the media and to shape news coverage. That has led to considerable debate in some nations over "spin doctors"—and in all nations over the nature of the relationship between citizens and their government.[5] The puzzle not only is how to hold government officials accountable for results that they cannot fully control. It is also about how to talk about the issue in an environment in which most of what citizens know comes through a medium that struggles to capture, with little success, the complex workings of public institutions.

Critical Issues in Governance

The global public management revolution has highlighted several critical issues that governments must solve—as well as eternal issues that have become far more central.

Nontraditional Service Delivery

A recurring theme of the global government reform movement is the growth of nontraditional, nonhierarchical, and often nongovernmental approaches to service delivery. Of course, governments have long relied on nongovernmental partners. In the United States, the use of non-governmental partners has become an essential and perhaps irreversible part of the governance system. Other nations, drawn by the impressive success of welfare reform and by the prospect of achieving greater productivity and more flexibility through nongovernmental partners, are following the American lead. In the twenty-first century, government will become increasingly reliant on nongovernmental partners for service delivery and those partners will depend more on government as an important source of their revenue stream. That interdependence will create new challenges to the institutional integrity and operating effectiveness of both parties.

More Decentralization of Government

Pushing operating responsibility to lower levels of government has become a central premise of many government reforms. Sweden has devolved health care programs to local governments. The United Kingdom has devolved most domestic responsibilities to new parliaments in Scotland and Wales. Even relatively centralized and bureaucratized governments such as in South Korea and Japan are considering more devolution. In the years ahead, government is likely to devolve yet more policy-making and management responsibility to lower levels. For federal systems, decentralization will bring new challenges in sorting out governmental roles; for unitary systems, it will bring even greater challenges in determining who is responsible for what.

Increased Burden of Service Coordination

From the British strategies of one-stop shopping to the extensive American program of customer service, governments increasingly are seeking to improve the coordination of their services. Indeed, one major negative side effect of the agency-based reforms in the Westminster countries is the fragmentation of service delivery. Agencies typically have strong incentives to look after their own programs and weak incentives to work with other agencies even though they serve the same citizens. Even in the United States, where cross-unit, cross-government work is common, drawing managers out of their tunnels to adopt a bottom-up view of service integration is difficult indeed. Governance in the twenty-first century certainly requires efforts to strengthen the ability of government organizations to manage more effectively. Just as important, it requires increasing the ability and incentives of government managers to work across their organizational boundaries to make government and its services more seamless and transparent to citizens.

Growing Globalization

The rise of the global economy, rapid spread of social problems, and international terrorism underline an inescapable reality of the twenty-first century: governments can no longer operate alone. Cooperation and coordination are the name of the game. The multinational force that fought in Bosnia required the approval of all the participating governments on everything from broad strategy to specific bombing targets. Though much criticized, the International Monetary Fund played a critical role in attacking the financial crisis in Southeast Asia, and the World Bank has led a strong campaign for reform as part of its strategy for aiding developing nations. When Coca-Cola's bottled beverages in Belgium were contaminated, it found itself dealing primarily with the European Union's food regulations. Globalization has become more than a watchword. It is unquestionably a central tenet of governance in the twenty-first century: although national governments maintain their sovereignty, they also must involve multinational organizations and other nation-states in decisionmaking on important issues. Moreover, multinational organizations—the International Monetary Fund, the World Bank, the United Nations, the European Union, and others—must carefully define their new roles in the global system of governance and develop the necessary capacity to play their roles effectively.

A report of the American National Intelligence Council's 2020 Project, which sought to look at the issues that governments will face in the years ahead, reached a clear conclusion. "At no time since the formation of the Western alliance system in 1949 have the shape and nature of international alignments been in such a state of flux." Indeed, the report argued, "We see globalization—growing interconnectedness reflected in the expanded flows of information, technology, capital, goods, services, and people throughout the world—as an overarching 'mega-trend,' a force so ubiquitous that it will substantially shape all the other major trends in the world of 2020."[6] If there is any sure bet to place on the future of public management reform, it is that it will continue—and that globalization will be the central problem it will need to address.[7]

The Role of National Government

A prophetic column by Daniel Bell that appeared in the *Washington Post* in January 1988 focuses the big issues sharply:

> The problem is a mismatch of governmental responsibilities and structures. Over time problems have tended, sloppily but steadily, to sort themselves out to the level of government best equipped to handle them. Programs that require adaptation to local needs, such as welfare reform, have tended to flow down to local governments. Programs that require multinational cooperation, such as trade policy and peacekeeping, have tended to flow up to international organizations and ad hoc international coalitions.[8]

This gradual accommodation of problems by institutions is only partially under way. At best, a generation of uneasy adaptation lies ahead. Moreover, the fundamental question remains left unanswered: if more policy problems are flowing down to subnational governments and up to multistate organizational forms, what will be the nation-state's role in governance in the twenty-first century? And what capacity does it need to play its role effectively? Is there sufficient intellectual capital to help policy makers wrestle with these challenges?

Government will need to be centrally involved in at least five key tasks:

—*Managing basic functions.* Central governments will need to continue to provide for the common defense, conduct foreign policy, and perform the other basic functions that define a nation.

—*Redistributing income.* Governments have taken very different views on just how much redistribution is desirable. Regardless of the level of redistribution, low-level governments cannot perform it adequately. Redistribution requires a broad base. With an increasingly aging population and with budget constraints growing, policymakers face an ever more difficult challenge.

—*Gathering data and promoting information-based links.* There is a fundamental paradox in the rapid spread of microcomputers. Although it has democratized information technology much more than in the days of large mainframe computers, communicating effectively across these related systems requires careful planning to ensure seamless integration. Such systems feed off large volumes of data that must be gathered in uniform ways to be effective. Thus central governments have an important role to play in making communication in the information age work.

—*Building bridges.* Management reforms depend heavily on new, close relationships among different government bureaucracies and between government and civil society. Central governments will have to play an integrative role to ensure delivery of effective public services.

—*Thinking strategically.* To cope with everything from workforce planning to next-generation technology, societies will need institutions that think strategically and shape the investments required to make cutting-edge systems work. It might be asking too much to expect such strategic thinking to happen spontaneously in the market.

Reform and Governance

The lessons of the global management reform movement are that
    —performing the five key tasks described above is essential
    —government, especially central government, must play an effective role in completing those tasks
    —performing the tasks often requires different skills of government managers, different processes in government, and sometimes new institutions to ensure that those processes work well.

If governments are to apply these lessons, they will need to maintain the instinct for reform in all their operations and to focus that instinct on building capacity to meet the challenges that lie ahead. Reform and reinvention are likely to become standard practice for governments of all stripes. Jocelyne Bourgon, Canada's clerk of the Privy Council and secretary to the Cabinet, asked whether governments have only scratched the surface of this challenge:

> And could it be that we all need to do much more to achieve the full potential of reinventing government, and to achieve the full potential of a modern society, a modern society which is a knowledge economy and a knowledge society, where we want both the fullness and the richness of a market economic system and the fullness and the richness of a democratic society coming together for the benefit of all citizens?[9]

Management reform for the twenty-first century will require the instinct for reform to become hardwired into the practice of government. Ultimately, this strategy means coupling the reform impulse with governance—government's increasingly important relationship with civil society and the institutions that shape modern life.

Notes

Chapter One

1. See, for example, Organization for Economic Cooperation and Development (OECD), *Managing across Levels of Government* (Paris, 1997), p. 15; and Michael Keating, *Public Management Reform and Economic and Social Development* (Paris: OECD, 1998), pp. 13, 54.

2. Comments at a meeting of the Public Governance Committee of the Organization for Economic Cooperation and Development, Paris, October 28, 2004.

3. See Christopher Pollitt and Geert Bouckaert, *Public Management Reform: A Comparative Analysis* (Oxford University Press, 2000).

Chapter Two

1. The seminal work of this movement was a paper by R. H. Coase, "The Nature of the Firm," *Economica* 4, no. 16 (1937): 386–405.

2. The literature on the New Zealand reforms is vast. Of special help, in addition to Allen Schick's analysis, *The Spirit of Reform: Managing the New Zealand State Sector in a Time of Change* (Wellington: New Zealand State Services Commission, 1996), are the following works: June Pallot, *Central State Government Reforms: Report on New Zealand* (Berlin: Central State Government Reforms Project, 1999); Colin James, *The State Ten Years On from the Reforms* (Wellington: New Zealand State Services Commission, 1998); Graham Scott, Ian Ball, and Tony Dale, "New Zealand's Public Management Reform: Implications for the United States," *Journal of Policy Analysis and Management* 16, no. 3 (1997): 357–81; Jonathan Boston and June Pallot, "Linking Strategy and Performance: Developments in the New Zealand Public Sector," *Journal of Policy Analysis and Management* 16, no. 3 (1997): 382–404; Jonathan Boston and others, *Public Management: The New Zealand Model* (Oxford University Press, 1996).

3. Schick, *The Spirit of Reform*, p. 12 (www.ssc.govt.nz/display/document .asp?docid=2845 [April 13, 2005]).

4. For a discussion of the transaction cost approach to economics, see Oliver E. Williamson, "The Economics of Organization: The Transaction Cost Approach," *American Journal of Sociology* 87, no. 3 (1981): 548–77.

5. Scott, Ball, and Dale, "New Zealand's Public Management Reform," p. 360. See also Malcolm Bale and Tony Dale, "Public Sector Reform in New Zealand and Its Relevance to Developing Countries," *The World Bank Research Observer* 13, no. 1 (1998): 117–19; and Jonathan Boston and others, eds., *Reshaping the State: New Zealand's Bureaucratic Revolution* (Oxford University Press, 1991). On principal-agent theory, see James Buchanan and Gordon Tullock, *The Calculus of Consent: Logical Foundations of Constitutional Democracy* (University of Michigan Press, 1962); Mancur Olson, *The Logic of Collective Action* (Harvard University Press, 1965); Gordon Tullock, *The Politics of Bureaucracy* (Washington: Public Affairs Press, 1965); William Niskanen, *Bureaucracy and Representative Government* (Chicago: Aldine Atherton, 1971); and Terry Moe, "The New Economics of Organizations," *American Journal of Political Science* 28 (November 1984): 739–75.

6. Schick, *The Spirit of Reform*.

7. Pallot, *Central State Government Reforms*.

8. Boston and others, *Public Management*.

9. Schick, *The Spirit of Reform*.

10. Wayne Thompson, "Cave Creek Haunts Survivor," *New Zealand Herald*, March 18, 2005 (www.nzherald.co.nz/index.cfm?ObjectID=10115932 [March 20, 2005]).

11. Quoted in Richard Norman, "Recovering from a Tidal Wave: New Directions for Performance Management in New Zealand's Public Sector," Victoria University, 2004, p. 6.

12. New Zealand State Services Commission, *Doing the Right Things and Doing Them Right: Improving Evaluative Activity in the New Zealand State Sector*, September 2003 (www.ssc.govt.nz/display/document.asp?docid=3506 [March 20, 2005]).

13. Office of the Minister of State Services, "Review of the Centre: State Services Commissioner's Mandate," February 2003 (www.ssc.govt.nz/upload/ downloadable_files/roc-sscers-mandate.pdf [March 20, 2005]).

14. Norman, "Recovering from a Tidal Wave." See also Richard Norman, "Managing through Measurement or Meaning? Lessons from Experience with New Zealand's Public Sector Performance Management Systems," *International Review of Administrative Sciences* 68 (December 2002): 619–28.

15. For a comparison, see Donald F. Kettl, "The Global Revolution in Public Management: Driving Themes, Missing Links," *Journal of Policy Analysis and Management* 16 (Summer 1997): 446–62. The Australian reforms are described in Australian Public Service Commission, *A Framework for Human Resource Management in the Australian Public Service*, 2nd ed. (Canberra: 1995). More generally, see David Osborne and Peter Plastrik, *Banishing Bureaucracy: The*

Five Strategies for Reinventing Government (Reading, Mass.: Addison-Wesley, 1997).

16. See Peter Aucoin, *The New Public Management: Canada in Comparative Perspective* (Montreal: Institute for Research on Public Policy, 1995).

17. For an analysis, see Sandford Borins, "What the New Public Management Is Achieving: A Survey of Commonwealth Experience," in *Advances in International Comparative Public Management*, edited by Lawrence R. Jones, Kuno Schedler, and Stephen W. Wade, pp. 49–70 (Greenwich, Conn.: JAI Press, 1997); Christopher Pollitt, *Managerialism and the Public Services: The Anglo-American Experience* (Oxford: Basil Blackwell, 1990); Colin Campbell and Graham K. Wilson, *The End of Whitehall: Death of a Paradigm* (Oxford: Blackwell, 1995).

18. One of the best analyses of this movement is Christopher Hood, *The Art of the State: Culture, Rhetoric, and Public Management* (Oxford: Clarendon Press, 1998).

19. Pollitt, *Managerialism and the Public Services*, p. 1.

20. Laurence E. Lynn Jr., "The New Public Management as an International Phenomenon: A Skeptical View," in *Advances in International Comparative Public Management*, edited by Jones, Schedler, and Wade, p. 114.

21. Borins, "What the New Public Management Is Achieving," p. 65.

Chapter Three

1. Jeffrey L. Pressman and Aaron Wildavsky, *Implementation: How Great Expectations in Washington Are Dashed in Oakland; Or, Why It's Amazing That Federal Programs Work at All, This Being a Saga of the Economic Development Administration as Told by Two Sympathetic Observers Who Seek to Build Morals on a Foundation of Ruined Hopes* (University of California Press, 1973).

2. Daniel Patrick Moynihan, *Maximum Feasible Misunderstanding: Community Action in the War on Poverty* (New York: Macmillan, 1970).

3. Arthur M. Schlesinger Jr., *The Imperial Presidency* (Boston: Houghton Mifflin, 1973).

4. David B. Walker, *The Rebirth of Federalism: Slouching toward Washington*, 2nd ed. (Washington: CQ Press, 1999).

5. Paul C. Light, *The True Size of Government* (Brookings, 1999), pp. 1, 22–25.

6. David Osborne and Ted Gaebler, *Reinventing Government: How the Entrepreneurial Spirit Is Transforming the Public Sector from Schoolhouse to Statehouse, City Hall to the Pentagon* (Reading, Mass.: Addison-Wesley, 1992). Osborne used the book to outline a government reform strategy for the Clinton campaign manifesto in "Reinventing Government: Creating an Entrepreneurial Federal Establishment," in *Mandate for Change*, edited by Will Marshall and Martin Schram (Berkeley Books, 1993).

7. See Paul C. Light, *The Tides of Reform, 1945–1995* (Yale University Press, 1997).

8. Al Gore, *From Red Tape to Results: Creating a Government That Works Better and Costs Less* (Government Printing Office, 1993).

9. See, for example, Charles T. Goodsell, "Did NPR Reinvent Government Reform?" *Public Manager* 22 (Fall 1993), pp. 7–10; David Segal, "What's Wrong with the Gore Report," *Washington Monthly*, November 1993, pp. 18–23; and Ronald C. Moe, "The 'Reinventing Government' Exercise: Misinterpreting the Problem, Misjudging the Consequences," *Public Administration Review* 54 (March–April 1994), pp. 125–36. For a balanced analysis, see Peri E. Arnold, *Making the Managerial Presidency: Comprehensive Reorganization Planning, 1905–1996* (University Press of Kansas, 1998), especially chapter 12.

10. Peter Drucker, "*Really* Reinventing Government," *Atlantic Monthly*, February 1995, pp. 50, 52.

11. Bill Clinton and Al Gore, *Putting People First* (New York: Times Books, 1992), pp. 23–24. Quoted in Gore, *From Red Tape to Results*, p. i.

12. Gore, *From Red Tape to Results*.

13. For an explanation of this balance, see Elaine Ciulla Kamarck, "The Impact of Reinventing Government," *The Business of Government* (Fall 1999): pp. 18, 20 (Washington: PricewaterhouseCoopers Endowment for the Business of Government).

14. Memorandum from Al Gore to Heads of Executive Departments and Agencies, "Second Phase of the National Performance Review," January 3, 1995.

15. See Sydney J. Freedberg Jr., "Attention, Pentagon Shoppers!" *National Journal*, April 25, 1998, pp. 932–33; and General Accounting Office (GAO), *Acquisition Reform: Implementation of Key Aspects of the Federal Acquisitions Streamlining Act of 1994*, NSIAD98-81 (March 1998).

16. NPR Deputy Director Bob Stone, "Gore Official Discusses High-Impact Strategy," *GovExec Daily Briefing*, May 7, 1998 (www.govexec.com/dailyfed [January 19, 2000]).

17. For a sample of these arguments, see Al Gore, *Businesslike Government: Lessons Learned from America's Best Companies* (Government Printing Office, 1997).

18. See John J. DiIulio Jr., Gerald Garvey, and Donald F. Kettl, *Improving Government Performance: An Owner's Manual* (Brookings, 1993), p. 8. See also Taegan D. Goddard and Christopher Riback, *You Won—Now What? How Americans Can Make Democracy Work from City Hall to the White House* (Scribners, 1998); Arnold, *Making the Managerial Presidency*; and especially Light, *The Tides of Reform*.

19. Light, *The Tides of Reform*.

20. Patricia W. Ingraham, James R. Thompson, and Ronald P. Sanders, eds., *Transforming Government: Lessons from the Reinvention Laboratories* (San Francisco: Jossey-Bass, 1997).

21. Merit Systems Protection Board, *The Changing Federal Workforce: Employee Perspectives* (Government Printing Office, 1998), p. vi.

22. Ibid., pp. vi–vii.

23. *National Performance Review: Savings for NPR Recommendations Made in 1993 and 1995 as of October 15, 1997* (www.napawash.org/waiver/index.htm [January 19, 2000]).

24. GAO's assessment of the problem is presented in *Management Reform: Implementation of the National Performance Review's Recommendations*, OCG-95-1 (December 1994).

25. This number excludes employees of the U.S. Postal Service. See U.S. Office of Personnel Management, Office of Workforce Information, *Monthly Report of Federal Civilian Employment*, SF 113-A (January 26, 1998).

26. Ibid.

27. From the Office of Personnel Management Central Data Bank (www.opm.gov).

28. Paul C. Light, *Thickening Government: Federal Hierarchy and the Diffusion of Accountability* (Brookings, 1995).

29. See Hal Lancaster, "Middle Managers are Back—But Now They're 'High-Impact Players,'" *Wall Street Journal*, April 14, 1998, p. B1.

30. See Perri 6, *Holistic Government* (London: Demos, 1997).

31. Mary Bryna Sanger, *The Welfare Marketplace: Privatization and Welfare Reform* (Brookings, 2003).

32. Office of Management and Budget, *President's Management Agenda* (GPO, 2001), p. 4 (www.whitehouse.gov/omb/budget/fy2002/mgmt.pdf [April 13, 2005]).

33. Amelia Gruber, "Nine Agencies Earn Higher Management Grades," Govexec.com, July 14, 2003 (www.govexec.com/dailyfed/0703/071403a1.htm [July 18, 2003]).

Chapter Four

1. See Herbert Kaufman, *Red Tape: Its Origins, Uses, and Abuses* (Brookings, 1977).

2. See William Niskanen, *Bureaucracy and Representative Government* (Chicago: Aldine Atherton, 1971).

3. For a comparison, see Kettl, "The Global Revolution in Public Management." This approach formed the core of the "reinventing government" arguments. See David Osborne and Ted Gaebler, *Reinventing Government: How the Entrepreneurial Spirit Is Transforming the Public Sector from Schoolhouse to Statehouse, City Hall to the Pentagon* (Reading, Mass.: Addison-Wesley, 1992); and David Osborne and Peter Plastrik, *Banishing Bureaucracy: The Five Strategies for Reinventing Government* (Reading, Mass.: Addison-Wesley, 1997).

4. See Paul C. Light, *The True Size of Government* (Brookings, 1999).

5. For an examination of the tools of government, see Lester M. Salamon and Odus V. Elliott, *The Tools of Government: A Guide to the New Governance* (New York: Oxford University Press, 2002); Donald F. Kettl, *Government by Proxy: (Mis?) Managing Federal Programs* (Washington: Congressional Quarterly Press,

1988); Frederick C. Mosher, "The Changing Responsibilities and Tactics of the Federal Government," *Public Administration Review* 40 (November–December 1980): 541–48; and H. Brinton Milward, "The Changing Character of the Public Sector," in *Handbook of Public Administration*, edited by James L. Perry (San Francisco: Jossey-Bass, 1996), pp. 77–95.

6. See the OECD website (www.oecd.org).

7. Al Gore, *The Best Kept Secrets in Government* (GPO, 1996).

8. Treasury Board of Canada, *Getting Government Right: Governing for Canadians* (Ottawa: 1997), pp. 11–15.

9. Prime Minister Tony Blair, *Modernising Government* (London: The Stationery Office, 1999).

10. Susie Stewart, ed., *The Possible Scot: Making Healthy Public Policy* (Edinburgh: Scottish Council Foundation, 1998); Graham Leicester and Peter Mackay, *Holistic Government: Options for a Devolved Scotland* (Edinburgh: Scottish Council Foundation, 1998). More generally, see Perri 6, *Holistic Government* (London: Demos, 1997).

11. Harold Seidman, *Politics, Position, and Power: The Dynamics of Federal Organization* (Oxford University Press, 1998), p. 142.

12. For an analysis of the Canadian reforms, see Sandford Borins, "New Public Management, Canadian Style," University of Toronto, 1999; and Peter Aucoin, *The New Public Management: Canada in Comparative Perspective* (Montreal: Institute for Research on Public Policy, 1995).

13. See Michael Keating, *Public Management Reform and Economic and Social Development* (Paris: OECD, 1998), pp. 18–19.

14. See OECD, *Performance Pay Schemes for Public Sector Managers: An Evaluation of the Impacts* (Paris, 1997), p. 64. The five countries surveyed were Australia, Denmark, Ireland, the United Kingdom, and the United States.

15. Ibid., p. 7.

16. See Patricia Ingraham, Helen Murlis, and B. Guy Peters, *The State of the Higher Civil Service after Reform: Britain, Canada and the United States* (Paris: OECD, 1999); and National Research Council, *Pay for Performance: Evaluating Performance Appraisal and Merit Pay* (National Academy Press, 1991).

17. OECD, *Performance Pay Schemes for Public Sector Managers*, p. 8.

18. National Partnership for Reinventing Government (NPR), *Balancing Measures: Best Practices in Performance Management* (Washington, 1999).

19. The best analysis of these forces is E. S. Savas, *Privatization and Public-Private Partnerships* (Chatham, N.J.: Chatham House Publishers, 2000).

20. Keating, *Public Management Reform and Economic and Social Development*, p. 70.

21. Ibid., p. 29.

22. Allen Hepner, *Examining Contestability in the APS [Australian Public Service]: Initial Information* (Canberra: Resource Management Improvement Branch, Department of Finance, 1995) (www.dofa.gov.au/pubs/pig/contest/contes02.htm [January 19, 2000]).

23. Ibid.

24. Jim Flanagan and Susan Perkins, "Public/Private Competition in the City of Phoenix, Arizona," *Government Finance Review* 11 (June 1995): 7–12.

25. See Savas, *Privatization and Public-Private Partnerships*, pp. 178–79.

26. Donald F. Kettl, *Sharing Power: Public Governance and Private Markets* (Brookings, 1993).

27. Hepner, *Examining Contestability in the APS.*

28. Global Forum on Reinventing Government, Washington, D.C., January 1–15, 1999, plenary session 1, January 14. The forum was cosponsored by the Innovations in American Government Program, Kennedy School of Government, Harvard University; the Innovations in Government Program, the Ford Foundation; the World Bank; the Inter-American Development Bank; the Organization for Economic Cooperation and Development; the National Partnership for Reinventing Government; the Office of Management and Budget; the Brookings Institution; and the United States Information Agency.

29. Bill Clinton and Al Gore, *Putting Customers First '95: Standards for Serving the American People* (Government Printing Office, 1995). pp. 1–2.

30. Gore, *The Best Kept Secrets in Government*, p. 33.

31. Keating, *Public Management Reform and Economic and Social Development*, p. 23.

32. *OECD Focus* (www.oecd.org/puma/focus/compend/it.htm [January 19, 2000]).

33. *OECD Focus* (www.oecd.org/puma/focus/compend/fr.htm [January 19, 2000]).

34. Zola Skweyiya, Minister of Public Service and Administration, South Africa, Global Forum, plenary session 1, January 14, 1999.

35. Keating, *Public Management Reform and Economic and Social Development*, p. 25.

36. See, for example, H. George Frederickson, "Painting Bull's Eyes around Bullet Holes," *Governing*, October 1992, p. 13; Ronald C. Moe, "Let's Rediscover Government, Not Reinvent It," *Government Executive*, June 1993, pp. 46–48, 60; and David Rosenbloom, "Have an Administrative Rx? Don't Forget the Politics," *Public Administration Review* 53 (November–December 1994): 503–07.

37. *American Customer Satisfaction Index: Federal Agencies Government-Wide Customer Satisfaction Report for the General Services Administration* (University of Michigan Business School, American Society for Quality, and Arthur Andersen, December 1999), especially pp. 3, 4.

38. OECD, *Information Technology as an Instrument of Public Management Reform: A Study of Five OECD Countries* (Paris, 1998), p. 11.

39. Rebecca Smith, "State Welfare Payments Going the Electronic Route; Debit Cards to Dispense Food Stamps, Benefits," *San Francisco Chronicle*, August 18, 1999, p. A1.

40. Martin Gallagher, European project manager and coordinator for the Card Link project in Europe and finance director of the Dublin Eastern Health Board, Global Forum, plenary session 2, January 15, 1999.

41. OECD, *Information Technology as an Instrument of Public Management Reform*, p. 5.

42. OECD, *The OECD Report on Regulatory Reform* (Paris, 1997), table 2.

43. Ibid., "Introduction" (www.oecd.org/subject/regreform/report.htm# Introduction [January 19, 2000]).

44. Prime Minister Jenny Shipley, Global Forum, opening plenary session, January 14, 1999.

Chapter Five

1. Lisa Getter, "GAO Report Disputes Gore Claims on Red-Tape Cuts," *Los Angeles Times*, August 14, 1999, p. 6.

2. Michael Keating, *Public Management Reform and Economic and Social Development* (Paris: OECD, 1998), p. 32.

3. See Joseph S. Nye, Philip D. Zelikow, and David C. King, eds., *Why People Don't Trust Government* (Harvard University Press, 1997).

4. See the analysis in "Is There a Crisis?" *Economist* (July 17, 1999), pp. 49–50.

5. Ibid.

6. Pippa Norris, "Mapping Political Support in the 1990s: A Global Analysis," in *Critical Citizens: Global Support for Democratic Governance*, edited by Pippa Norris (Oxford University Press, 1999), chapter 2.

7. Allen Schick, "Why Most Developing Countries Should Not Try New Zealand's Reforms," *World Bank Research Observer* 1 (February 1998): 124.

8. Ibid.

9. Global Forum on Reinventing Government, Washington, D.C., January 1–15, 1999, luncheon address, January 14.

10. Ibid., January 15, 1999.

11. Schick, "Why Most Developing Countries Should Not Try New Zealand's Reforms," pp. 127–28.

12. Ibid., p. 131.

13. Global Forum, plenary session 3, January 15, 1999.

14. Global Forum, luncheon address, January 14, 1999.

15. Global Forum, plenary session 3, January 15, 1999.

16. Graham Scott's presentation at the Global Forum, plenary session 1, January 14, 1999, contained a perceptive discussion of this issue.

17. Ibid.

18. Al Gore, *Businesslike Government: Lessons Learned from America's Best Companies* (GPO, 1997).

19. David Osborne and Ted Gaebler, *Reinventing Government: How the Entrepreneurial Spirit Is Transforming the Public Sector from Schoolhouse to Statehouse, City Hall to the Pentagon* (Reading, Mass.: Addison-Wesley, 1992).

20. For a powerful critique of the "borrowing" of reform ideas, see John Micklethwait and Adrian Wooldridge, *The Witch Doctors: Making Sense of the Management Gurus* (New York: Times Books, 1996), especially chapter 13.

Chapter Six

1. This chapter draws heavily on discussion at a meeting of the Public Governance Committee of the Organization for Economic Cooperation and Development, Paris, October 28, 2004.

2. Global Forum on Reinventing Government, Washington, D.C., January 1–15, 1999, luncheon speech, January 14.

3. Christopher Pollitt, "Performance Information for Democracy: The Missing Link," paper prepared for the Sixth Conference of the European Evaluation Society, Berlin, October 2004.

4. U.S. Government Accountability Office, *Performance Budgeting: Efforts to Restructure Budgets to Better Align Resources with Performance*, Report GAO-05-117SP (February 2005), pp. 7–8, and "Highlights" section.

5. For one example, see the report by the Danish Ministry of Finance, *Civil Service Advice and Assistance*, Report 1443, English summary (Albertslund: Schultz Information, 2004), at www.fm.dk.

6. National Intelligence Council, *Mapping the Global Future* (Washington: Government Printing Office, 2004), pp. 9–10.

7. Indeed, David Osborne has continued his work charting the direction of public management reform in a book with Peter Hutchinson, *The Price of Government: Getting the Results We Need in an Age of Permanent Fiscal Crisis* (New York: Basic Books, 2004).

8. Daniel Bell, "Previewing Planet Earth in 2013," *Washington Post*, January 3, 1988, p. B3.

9. Global Forum, plenary session 3, January 15, 1999.

Index

Accountability: importance, 53; issues, 15; of managers, 13, 14, 75, 79; as reform component, 2, 13, 14, 15, 85

Accounting: accrual, 13–14, 46–47; cash, 13, 47. *See also* Budgets

Administration. *See* Bureaucracy; Public management

Air Force Materiel Command, 26

Alternative service delivery, 45, 86. *See also* Outsourcing

American National Intelligence Council, *2020* Project, 87

American-style reforms, 9; Bush management agenda, 37–39, 73, 83–84; comparison to Westminster-style reforms, 39–40, 43, 75–76; convergence with Westminster-style reforms, 72–75, 76; decentralization, 43; goals, 72; governance issues, 42–44; history, 19–22, 27, 33–34. *See also* Reinventing government initiative

Armey, Dick, 34

Asian financial crisis, 4, 69, 87

Australia: customer service improvements, 52; Defence Commercial Support Program, 50; federal system, 74, 76; outsourcing, 49, 50; partnership of federal and state governments, 48; pay-for-performance system, 47; portfolio budgeting, 46; reforms, 16, 42; size of government, 62; uses of information technology, 55

Australia Post, 50

Autonomy, of government departments, 18

Ballivain, Amparo, 71

Belgium: contaminated Coca-Cola products, 87; customer service improvements, 52

Bell, Daniel, 88

"Big bang" reforms, 80, 81

Blair, Tony, 17

Bolivia, reforms, 71

Borins, Sandford, 18

Bosnia, multinational force, 87

Bourgon, Jocelyne, 71, 89

Britain. *See* United Kingdom

Budgets: accrual accounting, 13–14, 46–47; cash accounting, 13, 47; cost savings from reforms, 26, 28, 32, 49, 50, 60–61, 62, 83; Defense Department planning, programming, and budgeting system,